# Economic Crisis and Austerity in Southern Europe

Southern Europe has been hit hard by the global economic crisis and, as such, their welfare states have come under acute strain. Unmet need has sharply increased while significant welfare reforms and deep social spending cuts have been prominent in the crisis management solutions implemented by governments, labouring under EU constraints and the strict rescue-deal requirements for Greece and Portugal.

This volume provides a systematic comparative appraisal of welfare-state reform trajectories across Southern Europe prior to and during the crisis, and traces the impact of austerity policies and wider recession upon income inequality and poverty. It brings together a number of cross-country studies on major social policy areas, raising crucial questions. What policy choices are driving reforms as Southern European economies work their way out of fiscal difficulty? Can the crisis provoke the improvement of institutional capabilities and recalibration of social welfare? Or, instead, does structural adjustment indicate a significant policy turn towards the erosion of social rights? The contributions critically approach these issues and bring evidence to bear upon whether Southern European welfare capitalisms are becoming more dissimilar.

This book was originally published as a special issue of *South European Society and Politics*.

**Maria Petmesidou** is Professor of Social Policy at Democritus University of Thrace, Greece. She is a fellow of Comparative Research Programme on Poverty (CROP) of the International Social Science Council.

**Ana M. Guillén** is Professor of Sociology at the University of Oviedo, Spain. She is co-chair of Espanet-Spain.

# South European Society and Politics series

Series editors

*Susannah Verney, University of Athens, Greece*
*Anna Bosco, University of Trieste, Italy*

The parallel regime transitions of the 1970s, when Southern Europe was the vanguard of the 'third wave' of democratisation, the impact of EU membership and Europeanisation and more recently, the region's central role in the eurozone crisis have all made Southern Europe a distinctive area of interest for social science scholars. The *South European Society and Politics* book series promotes new empirical research into the domestic politics and society of South European states. The series, open to a broad range of social science approaches, offers comparative thematic volumes covering the region as a whole and on occasion, innovative single-country studies. Its geographical scope includes both 'old' and 'new' Southern Europe, defined as Italy, Greece, Portugal, Spain, Cyprus, Malta and Turkey.

**Economic Crisis and Austerity in Southern Europe: Threat or Opportunity for a Sustainable Welfare State?**
*Edited by Maria Petmesidou and Ana Marta Guillén*

**Southern Europe and the Financial Earthquake**
Coping with the First Phase of the International Crisis
*Edited by Susannah Verney, Anna Bosco and Marina Costa Lobo*

**Europeanisation of Public Policy in Southern Europe**
Comparative Political Economy from the 2000s to the Crisis
*Edited by Canan Balkir, H. Tolga Bolukbasi and Ebru Ertugal*

**Transformations of the Radical Left in Southern Europe**
Bringing Society Back In?
*Edited by Myrto Tsakatika and Marco Lisi*

**Elections in Hard Times: Southern Europe 2010-11**
*Edited by Anna Bosco and Susannah Verney*

**Voters and Parties in the Spanish Political Space**
*Edited by Ignacio Sánchez-Cuenca and Elias Dinas*

**New and Alternative Movements in Spain**
The Left, Identity and Globalizing Processes
*Edited by John Karamichas*

**Protest Elections and Challenger Parties**
*Edited by Susannah Verney and Anna Bosco*

**Previously published in the journal *South European Society and Politics***

**Europeanization and the Southern Periphery**
*Edited by Kevin Featherstone and George Kazamias*

# Economic Crisis and Austerity in Southern Europe

Threat or Opportunity for a
Sustainable Welfare State

*Edited by*
**Maria Petmesidou and
Ana M. Guillén**

LONDON AND NEW YORK

First published 2015
by Routledge

2 Park Square, Milton Park, Abingdon, Oxon OX14 4RN
711 Third Avenue, New York, NY 10017, USA

*Routledge is an imprint of the Taylor & Francis Group, an informa business*

First issued in paperback 2017

*British Library Cataloguing in Publication Data*
A catalogue record for this book is available from the British Library

ISBN 13: 978-1-138-85355-3 (hbk)
ISBN 13: 978-1-138-05951-1 (pbk)

Typeset in Minion
by RefineCatch Limited, Bungay, Suffolk

**Publisher's Note**
The publisher accepts responsibility for any inconsistencies that may have
arisen during the conversion of this book from journal articles to book chapters,
namely the possible inclusion of journal terminology.

**Disclaimer**
Every effort has been made to contact copyright holders for their permission to
reprint material in this book. The publishers would be grateful to hear from any
copyright holder who is not here acknowledged and will undertake to rectify
any errors or omissions in future editions of this book.

# Contents

# Citation Information

The chapters in this book were originally published in the *South European Society and Politics*, volume 19, issue 3 (September 2014). When citing this material, please use the original page numbering for each article, as follows:

**Chapter 1**
*Can the Welfare State as We Know It Survive? A View from the Crisis-Ridden South European Periphery*
Maria Petmesidou and Ana M. Guillén
*South European Society and Politics*, volume 19, issue 3 (September 2014) pp. 295–308

**Chapter 2**
*Reassessing South European Pensions after the Crisis: Evidence from Two Decades of Reforms*
David Natali and Furio Stamati
*South European Society and Politics*, volume 19, issue 3 (September 2014) pp. 309–330

**Chapter 3**
*South European Healthcare Systems under Harsh Austerity: A Progress–Regression Mix?*
Maria Petmesidou, Emmanuele Pavolini and Ana M. Guillén
*South European Society and Politics*, volume 19, issue 3 (September 2014) pp. 331–352

**Chapter 4**
*'Social Investment' or Back to 'Familism': The Impact of the Economic Crisis on Family and Care Policies in Italy and Spain*
Margarita León and Emmanuele Pavolini
*South European Society and Politics*, volume 19, issue 3 (September 2014) pp. 353–370

**Chapter 5**
*Welfare Performance in Southern Europe: Employment Crisis and Poverty Risk*
Rodolfo Gutiérrez
*South European Society and Politics*, volume 19, issue 3 (September 2014) pp. 371–392

**Chapter 6**

*The Distributional Impact of Austerity and the Recession in Southern Europe*
Manos Matsaganis and Chrysa Leventi
*South European Society and Politics*, volume 19, issue 3 (September 2014) pp. 393–412

Please direct any queries you may have about the citations to
clsuk.permissions@cengage.com

# Notes on Contributors

**Ana M. Guillén** is Professor of Sociology at the University of Oviedo, Spain, and is co-chair of Espanet-Spain. Her lines of research focus on comparative welfare state reform, Europeanisation of social policy, and quality of jobs. At present, she is directing a project on Reassessing Welfare Capitalism in South Europe (funded by the Spanish National Research Plan) and participating in other EC FP7 funded projects.

**Rodolfo Gutiérrez** is Professor of Sociology at the University of Oviedo, Spain, where he chaired the Department of Sociology from 2007 to 2012. He has published on the sociology of work and organisations, language and migration, socioeconomic inequality and poverty. He has co-edited *Working Poverty in Europe: A Comparative Approach* (Palgrave Macmillan, 2011).

**Margarita León** is a Senior Research Fellow at the Institute of Government and Public Policies (IGOP) of the Universitat Autònoma Barcelona. She has co-edited (with A.M. Guillén) *The Spanish Welfare State in European Context* (2011, Ashgate) and is the editor of the forthcoming book *The Transformation of Care in European Societies* (Palgrave, 2014).

**Chrysa Leventi** is a Senior Research Officer at the Institute for Social and Economic Research (ISER), University of Essex, and PhD candidate at the Department of International and European Economic Studies, Athens University of Economics and Business. Her research interests lie in the fields of tax–benefit microsimulation modelling for policy analysis, pension policy and reforms, and tax evasion.

**Manos Matsaganis** is an Associate Professor of European Social and Employment Policies at the Department of International and European Economics, Athens University of Economics and Business. He has published widely on the social impact of the economic crisis and the political economy of the welfare state in Greece and beyond. He is the coordinator of the Policy Analysis Research Unit (www.paru.gr).

**David Natali** is an Associate Professor at the University of Bologna in Forlì and a Professor on the PhD Programme in Political Science and Sociology at the Scuola Normale Superiore (SNS) of Pisa. He is senior researcher at the European Social Observatory, Brussels. He works on the comparative analysis of pension reforms, EU integration and social policies, and the study of industrial relations.

**Emmanuele Pavolini** is Associate Professor in Economic Sociology and Social Policy at the University of Macerata, Italy. His research interests include comparative welfare state research with a specific focus on social care and healthcare policies. Among his recent publications: (with C. Ranci) *Reforms in Long-Term Care Policies in Europe* (Springer, 2012) and (with A.M. Guillén) *Health Care Systems in Europe under Austerity* (2013, Palgrave).

**Maria Petmesidou** is Professor of Social Policy at Democritus University of Thrace, Greece, and a fellow of Comparative Research Programme on Poverty (CROP) of the International Social Science Council. She has published extensively on social policy and welfare reform in Greece and SE. Currently she is coordinating research on healthcare reform in Greece, and on policy learning and transfer in the field of youth employment policies (funded under the EC FP7 programme).

**Furio Stamati** is an MRes and PhD candidate at the European University Institute, Florence and a researcher at the European Social Observatory, Brussels. He works on the politics and political economy of pension and healthcare reform. His interests include economic history, the sociology of risk, and the relationship between welfare and democracy.

# Can the Welfare State as We Know It Survive? A View from the Crisis-Ridden South European Periphery

Maria Petmesidou and Ana M. Guillén

*South European countries have been hit hardest and longest by the post-2008 economic crisis. This has brought their welfare states under acute strain. Unmet need has sharply increased while significant welfare reforms and (more or less) deep cuts and changes in social spending have been prominent in the repertoire of the crisis management solutions implemented by the governments (under European Union constraints and the strict rescue-deal requirements for Greece and Portugal). This introduction briefly reviews reform trends prior to and during the crisis in order to highlight convergent and divergent paths among the four countries and outline the major questions addressed by the contributions to this volume.*

In the aftermath of the credit crunch, in a lecture Paul Pierson gave at the London School of Economics (LSE) (November 2010), he aptly raised the question of whether, after four decades of shifts and turns in social provision in the western world, the era of retrenchment *finally begins now* (see also Pierson 2011). This is mostly true for the South European (SE) welfare states that, contrary to the trajectory of northwest European welfare regimes, started expanding from the 1980s onwards, at a time of mounting pressure for retrenchment and restructuring in western countries, ushering in (particularly in the Anglo-Saxon world) a progressive politico-ideological weakening of welfare state legitimacy. During their 'lagged' path of welfare-state expansion, SE countries faced serious challenges from an array of internal and external pressures. Globalisation and, most importantly, mounting fiscal constraints in the run-up to the introduction of the Euro severely strained social budgets, even though unmet need and inequalities and imbalances in social protection persisted (though to a different extent among the four countries). Yet, more than ever before, the current financial and economic crisis has brought SE social protection systems to a critical juncture.

Since the early 1980s, institutional and policy change in European welfare states has been a central research theme. The accumulated literature throws light on the variety of reform strategies over the last four decades, in a macro-economic environment where Keynesian demand-side priorities gave way to stricter fiscal and monetary policy measures (culminating in the fiscal rules of the Economic and Monetary Union). In short, reform options embraced (a) cost-containment/retrenchment as a response to budgetary pressures, (b) employment-friendly measures in the field of tax/benefit systems so as to facilitate market participation; and (c) recalibration ('amending'/'modernising') of existing policy instruments in the face of new social risks of post-industrial societies (that is, changes in gender roles and family patterns, increasing female labour-force participation in the service economy, demographic ageing and rapid decline of lifetime jobs).

The latest crisis broke out in 2008 in SE and lasts to date. The credit crunch, turned into a sovereign debt crisis in SE, has intensified the challenges and tensions faced by the SE welfare states and brought to the fore questions such as: Has the crisis ushered in a period of draconian social retrenchment? Does this indicate a significant erosion of social and labour rights, as social policies in the broad sense have become the main variables of adjustment – through internal devaluation – in the European Union (EU) (Degryse, Jepsen & Pochet 2013)? Or is there, instead, a window of opportunity for recasting social policy along the lines of a 'social investment' welfare state (Hemerijck 2012)?

Equally relevant is Pierson's argument about tactics of policy 'drift' (e.g. continuous provision exhaustion) that may eventually outflank the welfare state, just as the 'Maginot Line', built on the eastern frontier of France to prevent Nazi invasion, failed to do so, as Pierson (2011, p. 22) aptly put it.[1] Surely, drastic budget austerity and an erosion of labour rights, all the more prevalent in Europe amidst the protracted aftershocks of the financial crisis, threaten to tip the balance away from social Europe. Crisis management measures (the 'Six Pack' of macroeconomic policies, the 'Euro Plus Pact', the 'European Semester' and the 'rescue deals' for the ailing countries) more or less embrace a single objective, namely structural adjustment through wage squeezes, weakening public services and social protection. This reflects the dominance of the market-driven convergence approach (via deregulation and market adjustments), given the fact that any plan for socio-political integration has persistently been undermined in the EU so far (Degryse, Jepsen & Pochet 2013). Advocacy in favour of an emerging 'social investment' paradigm does entail innovative potential to counteract the austerity orthodoxy. This is premised upon the development of preventive 'social investment' policies and the balancing of flexibility and security. Nonetheless, the influence of such a perspective has remained at an ideational level so far.

Against a backdrop of significant and rapid policy moves in Europe, the contributions to this volume aim to shed light on reform trends in major social policy fields in SE countries. The emphasis is on the policy options, the orientation and nature of reforms, the specific policy outputs and the ensuing parametric/ paradigmatic change, as well as the current (and potential) outcomes.

## Reform Paths Prior to the Crisis

Closely linked to the above considerations is the question of any structural changes in the recent past that may have significantly altered the hybrid form of welfare arrangements in SE countries, which has been a prevalent trait for a considerable time (Guillén & León 2011, pp. 1–16; Petmesidou 2013). These embrace elements from all three 'welfare regimes' distinguished by the well-known typology documented in the work of Esping-Andersen (1990). Pensions developed on an occupational basis according to the Bismarckian model. Traditionally, these were highly fragmented, but over the last two decades they have undergone significant changes in the direction of levelling out coverage and provision and introducing stronger actuarial components and private insurance (though varyingly among the four countries). In the late 1970s to the early 1980s, a social-democratic element was introduced in healthcare with the establishment of national healthcare systems. This is a significant path shift that, however, met with a different degree of success in each country. On the other hand, statutory coverage of care and social assistance needs has been limited and family arrangements have predominated. Non-governmental organisations (NGOs) (including religious organisations) contribute to welfare provision. A dense network has been prominent in the Latin Rim countries with the Catholic Church and the Red Cross playing a crucial role. This is not the case in the Balkan area where the values of Eastern Orthodoxy and its historical limitations of social activism did not provide fertile ground for institutionalised voluntary action (Petmesidou & Polyzoidis 2013).[2]

Under the influence of internal and external pressures (i.e. demographic trends, new social risks, changing gender roles, budgetary strains and the fiscal requirements for joining the European Monetary Union [EMU]) all four countries faced the need to contain costs and rationalise/modernise social programmes. From the mid-1990s, to one extent or another, EU influence introduced a novel discourse in SE countries on 'recalibrating' welfare programmes towards more active and service-oriented provision. The extent to which this has triggered reform that has altered the traditional configuration of social provision varies among the four countries. In the run-up to the adoption of the euro, reform gathered momentum in Italy and Portugal, but has waned since the early 2000s. Seemingly, in Spain, a piecemeal but steady process of negotiated reform has been a key characteristic of high-level policy-shaping decisions until recently (Guillén & Léon 2011). Compared with the other three countries, Greece ostensibly failed to deal with major dysfunctions and imbalances in social protection in the previous decades. The debilitating crisis made an overhaul imminent but at the same time it put the reform process in dire straits.

In Italy, it is largely the intense political crisis in the early 1990s (which swept away the existing party structure), as well as the challenges of joining the EMU, that gave an impetus to social reform and provided propitious conditions for social pacts around wide-ranging changes in social protection, industrial relations and labour market policies (Ferrera & Gualmini 2004). Public deficits and indebtedness soared dramatically during the 1980s in Italy (a characteristic also shared by Greece), partly because of a significant expansion of earnings-related schemes (proliferation of new funds, early retirement, disability pensions) under the strong grip of clientelistic–particularistic exchanges. Thus retrenchment and rationalisation in traditional policy fields (such as pensions) became a key priority in the 1990s, and were accompanied by significant steps forward in social assistance and social services, at least at the level of legislation and experimentation (e.g. legislation for the introduction of an anti-poverty scheme, piloted in selected municipalities between 1998 and 2002, and legal provisions for reducing regional inequalities and guaranteeing 'an essential level of service' throughout the country on the basis of universal though selective criteria; see Ferrera 2012). However, as extensively stressed in the literature (Sacchi & Bastagli 2005; Ascoli 2011; Hemerijck et al. 2013; Madama, Natili & Jessoula 2013), the 'recalibration momentum' significantly weakened in the early 2000s.[3] The reform setback highlighted the resilience of traditional patterns in social assistance. Moreover, as Madama, Natili and Jessoula argue (2013, p. 26), some new benefits in effect since the 1990s (e.g. a maternity allowance for uninsured mothers, benefit to families with more than three children, and support for low income tenants) have persistently been very low, hardly securing the family protection of low income and marginalised groups.

A steady process of negotiated reform started early in Spain, after the restoration of democracy. It effectively tackled fragmentation in pensions and healthcare, balanced actuarial criteria with improved coverage of less protected groups (workers with discontinuous contribution records, widows, orphans and others) and put social insurance on a sustainable track. It equally contributed to the overhaul of healthcare, culminating in the establishment of a devolved national health service (NHS). Particularly during the 2000s, until the eruption of the crisis, path-shifting 'recalibration' strategies in social care, gender mainstreaming and social assistance were pursued by both the conservative and socialist governments alternating in office. Among the key measures are the active integration income (in 2000), increased flexibility of maternity/paternity leave schemes, expansion of preschool childcare, progressive legislation on gender equality, and, just before the eruption of the crisis, the passing of legislation making social care for dependent people a social right (Guillén 2010).[4]

In Portugal the prospect of accession to the EU and, later on, the challenge of joining the EMU prompted consensual forms (through social pacts) of interconnected reforms in incomes, labour market, social security and welfare policies. The introduction of the RMI (minimum guaranteed income) and integrated 'social insertion' policies at a community level signpost a significant attempt to expand the field of social needs coverage. Yet, after entrance into the EMU, social pacting weakened and reform dynamism subsided.

In contrast, Greece hardly built any processes of negotiated reform in the previous decades. Focal actors (think tanks and policy communities) for driving policy debate were absent, decentralisation proceeded very slowly (with regard to social policies and programmes), and the scope of multilevel governance was limited (Petmesidou & Mossialos 2006; Petmesidou 2013). A tradition of statist–paternalistic forms of social organisation, closely linked with highly politicised, fragmented and conflictive industrial relations in this country, was persistently conducive to policy stalemates and reform impasses until the late 2000s.

Table 1 summarises the trends in total social spending and its main components, in the four countries, in the decades of the 1990s and 2000s until the crisis struck, and up to 2011 (for which disaggregated data are available). There is a noticeable trend of convergence of per capita social expenditure to the corresponding EU-15 average (measured in purchasing power standards, at constant 2005 prices) from 1990 until the late 2000s. But, particularly in Spain, Greece and Portugal, per capita (total) social spending did not improve as fast as per capita gross domestic product (GDP) (measured against the respective EU-15 average; see columns [6] to [11] in Table 1). This indicates that social expenditure has hardly 'grown to its limits' and casts doubts on the argument that welfare spending has been a major cause of the current fiscal woes of these countries. The last column of Table 1 depicts the percentage change of public social spending (in real terms) from 2007/08 to 2012/13. Strikingly, in the hardest-hit country (Greece) public social spending in real terms plunged by about 18 per cent, even though social needs enormously increased (during this time the unemployment rate almost tripled reaching about 27 per cent in June 2014, the highest rate in the EU;[5] see also the contributions by Matsaganis and Leventi and by Gutiérrez in this volume). By contrast, in Spain, which has equally recorded a rapid increase of unemployment since 2008, real public social spending rose by about 18 per cent. Smaller increases are observed in Portugal and Italy (by 4.3 and 3.7 per cent, respectively).

If we disaggregate spending by major categories, in Italy per capita expenditure on pension benefits has persistently been higher than the EU-15 average, indicating the resilience of the traditionally pension-heavy welfare state. In terms of per capita spending on healthcare services and sickness benefits, Spain and Italy moved closer to the EU-15 average over the 2000s, but the trend has reversed slightly since the eruption of the crisis. The distance of SE countries from the EU-15 average has been highest regarding per capita spending on family/children and social exclusion;[6] the gap slightly diminished between 2000 and 2008, but reversed afterwards.

In a nutshell, significant differences with respect to the roadmap and pacing of reform characterised the four countries in the two decades prior to the crisis. Spain seems to have steadily pursued a path of system rationalisation and 'retuning' geared towards gender equality and work–family balance. However, as stressed above, total social spending per capita in purchasing power standards (PPS) remained significantly below the EU-15 average. Italy has gone through periods of drastic reforms ushering in permanent retrenchment, market-based systems of organisation, and privatisation

**Table 1** Social Expenditure and GDP per Capita

| | Per capita expenditure by type of benefits (in PPS, EU-15 = 100) 2000/2008/2011 | | | | | Total social expenditure per capita (in PPS, EU-15 = 100) | | | GDP per capita | | | Per-centage change in real public social spending 2007/08–2012/13 |
|---|---|---|---|---|---|---|---|---|---|---|---|---|
| | Old age & survivors[a] (1) | Health/sickness & disability[b] (2) | Family/children[c] (3) | Unemploy-ment[d] (4) | Social exclusion[e] (5) | 2000[f] (6) | 2008 (7) | 2011 (8) | 2000 (9) | 2008 (10) | 2011/12 (11) | |
| Italy | 109/112/113 | 75/79/76 | 53/64/64 | 22/42/61 | 11/12 | 91 | 93 | 92 | 101 | 88 | 91/90 | +3.7% |
| Greece | 61/86/83 | 51/72/62 | 53/67/63 | 46/81/57 | 96/78 | 57 | 79 | 76 | 73 | 87 | 72/69 | −17.6% |
| Spain | 62/74/79 | 67/76/70 | 40/64/55 | 74/103/83 | 49/32 | 59 | 73 | 74 | 84 | 93 | 88/87 | +17.6% |
| Portugal | 47/68/71 | 61/59/54 | 31/42/38 | 48/41/40 | 42/40 | 52 | 60 | 61 | 68 | 66 | 71/69 | +4.3% |
| EU-15 | 100 | 100 | 100 | 100 | 100 | 100 | 100 | 100 | 100 | 100 | 100 | – |
| EU-27 | – | – | – | – | – | 85 | 88 | 89 | 87 | 90 | 91 | +10.7%[g] |

*Notes:* A note of caution is needed with regard to social exclusion spending (5). In Greece, this spending category embraces mostly EU-funded programmes targeted to specific measures (e.g. social inclusion measures for Roma, ethnic minorities and other vulnerable groups). These are often one-off programmes that have rarely led to the formation of permanent social service provision arrangements. Hence the persistently very low redistributive effect of social transfers (other than pensions) in Greece; see Dafermos and Papatheodorou (2011). Additionally, poor administrative capabilities in the country, perverse redistribution, and classification/measurement problems with regard to this spending category call for great caution in interpreting relevant data. Also, in the Italian case, expenditure on social exclusion may well be unreliable because of underestimation of regional and local spending in this area.
*Source:* Own calculations (Eurostat data) and Organisation for Economic Cooperation and Development (OECD) data retrieved from: http://www.oecd.org/els/societyataglance.htm

[a] Per capita expenditure (in PPS) is calculated for the population aged 60 years and over.
[b] Per capita expenditure (in PPS) is calculated for the total population.
[c] Per capita expenditure (in PPS) is calculated for the population under 20 years of age.
[d] Per capita expenditure (in PPS) is calculated for the total number of unemployed.
[e] Per capita expenditure (in PPS) is calculated for the population at risk of poverty and social exclusion.
[f] Data for 2000 based on the European Social Statistics Report 1996–2004.
[g] The average rate refers to the 21 European countries that are OECD members. As for public labour market policies (LMPs), in 2011 expenditure amounted to less than one per cent of GDP in Greece (active LMPs absorbed about 0.22 per cent of GDP), 3.71 per cent of GDP in Spain (active LMPs 0.88 per cent), 1.78 per cent of GDP in Italy (active LMPs 0.41 per cent) and 1.93 per cent of GDP in Portugal (active LMPs 0.59 per cent) (OECD database retrieved from: http://stats.oecd.org/).

(in major policy fields such as pensions and healthcare), balanced with considerable attempts to expand less developed areas (e.g. social services and social assistance). Yet, since the early 2000s, significant setbacks in the momentum of reform, compounded by serious obstacles in implementation (due to institutional stickiness and low capabilities), greatly limited the scope and effectiveness of reform.

Of the two smaller countries, Greece manifests a 'gridlocked' system. This is most clearly reflected in the persistently high poverty rate over the 1990s and 2000s, until the eve of the crisis (about 21 per cent, EU-15 average about 16 per cent), and the strikingly low redistributive effects of all other social transfers (except pensions; namely sickness, family, unemployment and social assistance benefits). In Portugal, some formative conjunctures (like for instance the mid to late 1990s) produced an attempt to expand social rights, but imbalances and fragmentation in traditional policy fields remained.

## Where is Reform Heading in SE under the Crisis?

It is primarily through public indebtedness that SE economies have been hit by the financial crisis. In Spain, both public deficit (showing a surplus in 2007) and public debt were comparatively very low at the onset of the crisis (60 per cent of GDP), but the eruption of the international credit crunch and massive private indebtedness (amounting to twice the national GDP) intensified contraction that had already started with the bursting of the construction bubble, a little prior to the global financial storm, putting an end to the outstanding economic and employment growth in the 2000s. In Italy and Portugal the financial turbulence precipitated economic decline that was all too evident prior to the crisis and triggered the ballooning of public debt and deficit. Greece exhibited significant rates of growth over the 2000s but profligate borrowing in order to fund the government budget and current account deficit, in tandem with weak revenue collection and structural rigidities of the economy, heightened vulnerability to the international financial turmoil. Soaring borrowing costs cut Greece and Portugal from money markets and brought them under a bailout deal with the International Monetary Fund (IMF), the European Commission and the European Central Bank (the so-called 'troika'). The two larger SE countries have so far avoided coming under the strict surveillance of a bailout deal, but they have also had to tread a harsh austerity path.

In the bailout countries the 'Memoranda of Understanding' (MoUs) signed under the rescue deals stipulated wholesale reforms and sweeping cuts in public spending (especially in Greece). Both countries are confronted with strong pressure to tackle major imbalances in the two traditional policy fields – pensions and health (wipe out fragmentation, equalise coverage and seek efficiency gains through market-based mechanisms of funding, organisation and delivery). Evidently, particularly in the case of Greece (but also in Portugal), the crisis is functioning as a catalyst for breaking system gridlocks. Major changes so far include an overhaul of pensions in Greece (from a pay-as-you-go to a multi-tier system favouring funded pension schemes and private savings), integration of health insurance, and health sector reform and redeployment. Similar reform options were included in the MoU for Portugal.

However, under conditions of a debilitating crisis, harsh austerity and repeatedly false forecasts by the troika as to the depth, duration and (social) effects of the slump, it is highly questionable whether the effects of reform will be successful in balancing drastic cuts with improvement in coverage, quality and equity, or whether, instead, a drift towards permanent retrenchment is imminent. So far, in the hardest-hit countries, substantial to severe cuts in benefits, in tandem with increasing direct and indirect taxes, foreclosures because of mortgage defaults, bankruptcies and waves of redundancies (in the private and public sector) have caused steadily rising hardship among large sections of low and middle income groups who fall into the ranks of the 'new poor'. Alarmingly, the financial crisis has turned into a deep and prolonged economic and social crisis. In Greece, under the two bailout programmes GDP shrank by a quarter between 2009 and 2013, while forecasts by national and some international bodies of a return to positive growth in 2014 (zero per cent to 0.6 per cent) do not allow much scope for optimism, as they continue to project a very anaemic trend over the longer term.[7] The possibility of a significant fiscal gap through 2015 and 2016 remains open, and fuels alternative scenarios about a protracted continuation of harsh austerity. A major question is how far drastic retrenchment and rapid rolling back of protection will dominate, dragging coverage down to the lowest common denominator.[8]

Spain is facing a significant and abrupt turning point. After a decade of ambitious social reforms and an expansionary trend, austerity and staggering unemployment are stress-testing the social protection system. The institutional structure remains almost intact but significantly diminishing coverage and system generosity (particularly with respect to newly consolidated social rights) may cancel out recent innovations, indicating a drift towards welfare state erosion. Also, internal divergence (increasing variation among autonomous communities) with respect to coverage, access, benefit generosity and the introduction of market-based mechanisms may seriously negatively affect welfare outcomes. Public social spending in real terms increased, as indicated above, but at the same time unmet need deepened (four out of ten unemployed people do not receive unemployment benefit and safety-net benefits amount to about half of the income level constituting the poverty line). Most significantly, both poverty among children and inequality have risen in an unprecedented upward trend. In Italy the crisis has intensified retrenchment, which was already the main orientation of reforms since the mid-1990s. The safety net has so far been meagre, poorly addressing rising risks (increasing long-term unemployment and poverty), and social transfers appear to be skewed towards the better-off more than in any other SE country.[9]

Most importantly, in all four countries reform agendas are pushed through that reduce labour protection, with the exception of increased coverage for unemployment in Italy. In general, they embrace the drastic reduction of collective bargaining and the weakening of unions, freezing and/or cuts in wages, and greater flexibility in the rules of hiring and dismissal of workers (including the duration of temporary and fixed-term contracts).

Is austerity taking away the foundations of 'Social Europe'? A set of values and goals ('social justice', 'equity' and 'solidarity') constitutive of the European Social Model and defining the basis of European identity seem to be fading away, and appeal to them has increasingly been undermined by the crisis management policies. Moreover, persistent austerity runs counter to the renewed objective of the EU 2020 Strategy to significantly reduce the number of poor in the current decade. Alarmingly, rising poverty and insecurity are not a phenomenon limited to the ailing countries. Recent data show that about 125 million people or 25 per cent of the EU population lived in poverty and/or social deprivation in 2012. Unemployment, old age and low wages are the main causes.

Cuts of an unprecedented magnitude accompany downward adjustment that heightens divergence and polarisations in socio-geographical terms. These conditions shake the very foundations of Social Europe. Whether this is an irreversible path towards permanent retrenchment and strain, even if and when the economic crisis is over, is an open question.[10] As the verdict is still out, the contributions to this volume aim to highlight major dimensions and components of social and labour market reform in the ailing SE periphery, which, under the imperative of the crisis, provides a vantage point for dissecting any decisive turns and shifts emerging from the clash between Europe's social ambitions (as inscribed in the Treaties) and European economic governance which is exerting dangerous downwards pressure on labour and social rights. Last but not least, SE welfare capitalism is becoming increasingly dissimilar in the four countries, putting into question the existence of a distinctive 'model'.

## The Contributions to the Volume

The first paper, by Natali and Stamati, comparatively reviews pension reform in SE countries over the last two decades. The authors trace the domestic political dynamics of reform in the four countries and examine the influence of EU convergence criteria and policy options under the impact of the crisis. Addressing the demographic problem in an economically viable way is paramount, as is also improving intergenerational justice and social redistribution. Evidently the crisis exerts heavy strains on the realignment of these objectives, and this brings to the fore serious long-run sustainability and adequacy questions. Major changes in the institutional set-up of pension systems (the changing public/private pension mix and the interplay between first pillar and supplementary schemes), and the distributional impact of the reforms are at the forefront of the analysis. The authors highlight the extent of diversity among the four SE countries prior to the crisis, and comparatively examine how the crisis is affecting reform roadmaps.

The contribution by Petmesidou, Pavolini and Guillén deals with similar questions by examining cross-country healthcare reform. The authors start with a brief review of how each system has evolved over the last two decades and comparatively discuss issues concerning system consolidation, funding and organisation. By drawing upon the available literature on welfare state retrenchment and restructuring, the authors attempt to map and explain reform trends under the imperative of the crisis. They critically examine the magnitude of fiscal constraint, the redeployment of public resources and personnel and the public–private boundary shifts across the four countries. Whether the crisis has shaken the universalist underpinnings of healthcare in the four countries is a crucial question. On the basis of available data so far, the authors provide a comparative assessment of the impact of the crisis and the austerity-driven reforms on current and expected policy outputs and outcomes with an emphasis on responsiveness to need, quality criteria, self-reported health status, and inequality.

León and Pavolini's analysis centres on the impact of the economic crisis on family policies in SE countries. As a welfare domain, family policies have traditionally been weak in these countries. For reasons that are related to the historical trajectory and the specific configuration of the SE welfare state, family policies have had a specific imprint and have remained well below averages in expenditure and coverage characterising the continental welfare states. In the last two decades, however, and with a major impulse from the process of European integration, some SE countries have created new family programmes and expanded existing ones. These changes have been accompanied by deep shifts in underlying cultural values and attitudes with regard to the role of women and equal parenting and were certainly influenced by processes of European convergence. However, policy innovation and 'path departure' have been critically undermined by current austerity plans.

The paper by Gutiérrez focuses on the deep employment crisis in SE triggered by the 'Great Recession', in relationship with the persistently weak social redistribution of SE welfare states. The author comparatively examines the magnitude and profile of the job crisis in the four countries and traces any convergence (or divergence) in labour market policy reforms over the last few years. Mainstream approaches to the economic malaise of SE countries emphasise 'inflexibilities' in the labour market as a main cause (although, for instance, over a third of labour contracts are fixed term in Spain). In this vein, strategies towards greater labour market flexibility and deregulation have been forcefully instigated by the 'rescue plans' in Greece and Portugal and largely adopted in Spain and Italy too. The paper brings evidence to bear upon diminishing employment protection and the dismantling of labour rights in tandem with increasing poverty risks and income inequality, and highlights the trajectory of each country in this respect.

In the last paper, Matsaganis and Leventi evaluate recent developments as regards the social impact of the crisis in Portugal, Spain, Italy and Greece. Given that official statistics tend to lag behind by two to three years, the authors apply the European tax–benefit model (European Microsimulation Model [EUROMOD]) to simulate recent changes. They trace the changing distribution of incomes under the impact of the crisis, and assess how (and to what extent) inequality and poverty have risen as a result of two interrelated factors: the austerity measures taken to reduce fiscal deficits and the wider recession causing business closures and job losses. The authors quantify the distributional impact of both of these factors and provide an estimate of how the total burden of the crisis is shared across income groups. They conclude with brief remarks on the policy implications of their research.

The present volume brings together a number of cross-country studies on major social policy areas in SE and is intended to provide valuable information and analytic insights to both academics and public decision-makers. Over the last few years there has been an increasing amount of literature on country-specific social policy studies in SE and on comparisons between selected countries in the area. By drawing upon this literature and including further research evidence and analyses, this volume aims to contribute to a systematic comparative appraisal of welfare-state reform trajectories across SE prior to and during the crisis. This is indeed a timely task, as SE is precisely one of the geographical areas where the crisis has hit longest and hardest within the EU. The volume is expected to enrich the critical dialogue on the consequences of austerity politics and policies that pressingly threaten the very idea of Social Europe and raise crucial questions with regard to the challenges ahead for the revitalisation of the social dimension of the EU.

## Acknowledgements

The work undertaken for this volume has benefited from funding by the Spanish National Research Plan (CABISE Project – Reassessing Welfare Capitalism in South Europe – CSO 2012-33976) and also by the Spanish Foundation for Science and Technology (FECYT, FCT-13-6137). We would like to thank Martin Rhodes for his valuable comments on earlier versions of the papers at the 21st Conference of Europeanists (Washington, March 2014). Our gratitude for really helpful comments and suggestions is also due to Maurizio Ferrera for acting as external reviewer for the whole special issue and to the anonymous referees who reviewed each article individually. The advice of the journal editors is also gratefully acknowledged.

## Notes

1. In this respect he considers the US to be the precursor for Europe, in a process where the middle and lower classes will face a tight squeeze (Hacker & Pierson 2010).
2. However, the deep economic and social crisis has heightened the need for a stronger involvement of the voluntary sector in social provision.
3. The Berlusconi governments discontinued the anti-poverty social insertion scheme and drastically cut funding for family support and social services. Apparently, the Prodi administration in office between 2006 and 2008 did not restore reform momentum for addressing new risks (Jessoula & Vesan 2011).
4. However, with respect to tackling labour market dualisation, no substantial progress was recorded until the eve of the crisis.
5. Unless otherwise stated, all statistics are taken from the Eurostat and OECD webpages accessed at: http://epp.eurostat.ec.europa.eu/ and http://www.oecd.org/social/soc/societyataglance.htm
6. With the exception of Greece (see caption of Table 1).
7. In Portugal GDP posted about 6.5 per cent contraction between 2011 and 2013. The country has formally exited its rescue programme but harsh austerity remains the mantra of the government.

8. Strikingly, EU authorities have been utterly oblivious of the vociferous criticism of the so-called SAPs (structural adjustment programmes) imposed by international financial institutions on a large number of over-indebted developing countries in the decades of the 1980s and 1990s, which dismantled even the rudimentary social protection institutions in these countries and intensified poverty and destitution (Greer 2013).

9. In 2010, in Italy social transfers to the lowest 30 per cent of income groups amounted to 56 per cent of average transfers, while those to the top 30 per cent of income groups amounted to 146 per cent of average transfers; on account of this inequality, Italy is ranked third among OECD countries (after Turkey and Mexico [source as in footnote five]).

10. European Union and national crisis management policy tools have provided fertile ground for the strengthening of the neoliberal project, in ideological, ethical and policy terms, in Europe (see, for instance, the contributions to the special issue of the Journal of Contemporary European Studies, vol. 22, no. 2, 2014, on Social Welfare and the Ethics of Austerity in Europe: Justice, Ideology and Equality). Yet, an imminent convergence to such a policy shift across Europe constitutes a contentious issue. Differing policy mixes in the different welfare regimes, and a sustained better performance of the Nordic countries in economic and social terms (e.g. Sweden's economy has fared through the crisis much better than other EU countries and the redistributive effect of its welfare state has remained comparatively strong), have kept alive the debate on the need to strengthen advocacy for an EU 'social investment pact'.

## References

Ascoli, U. (ed.) (2011) *Il Welfare in Italia*, Il Mulino, Bologna.

Dafermos, J. & Papatheodorou, Ch. (2011) 'Το παράδοξο της κοινωνικής πολιτικής στην Ελλάδα: γιατί η αύξηση των δαπανών για κοινωνική προστασία δεν μείωσε τη φτώχεια;' ['The paradox of social policy in Greece: why the increase of social expenditure has not reduced poverty'] Policy Paper, Observatory on Poverty, Incomes and Social Inequalities, INE-GSEE, available online at: http://www.ineobservatory.gr/sitefiles/books/pdf/report2.pdf

Degryse, C., Jepsen, M. & Pochet, P. (2013) 'The Euro Crisis and its impact on national and European social policies', ETUI Working Paper, Brussels.

Esping-Andersen, G. (1990) *The Three Worlds of Welfare Capitalism*, Polity Press, Oxford.

Ferrera, M. (2012) *Le politiche sociali. L'Italia in prospettiva comparata*, Il Mulino, Bologna.

Ferrera, M. & Gualmini, E. (2004) *Rescued by Europe?* Amsterdam University Press, Amsterdam.

Greer, S. (2013) '(Why) Did we forget about history? Lessons for the Eurozone from the failed conditionality debates in the 80s', OSE Research Paper No. 11, European Social Observatory, Brussels.

Guillén, A. M. (2010) 'Defrosting the Spanish welfare state: the weight of conservative components', in *A Long Good-Bye to Bismarck: The Politics of Welfare Reforms in Continental Welfare State*, ed. B. Palier, Amsterdam University Press, Amsterdam, pp. 183–206.

Guillén, A. M. & León, M. (2011) 'Introduction', in *The Spanish Welfare State in European Context*, eds A. Guillén & M. León, Ashgate, Aldershot, pp. 1–16.

Hacker, J. & Pierson, P. (2010) *Winner-Take-All Politics*, Simon & Schuster, New York.

Hemerijck, A. (2012) *Changing Welfare States*, Oxford University Press, Oxford.

Hemerijck, A., Dräbing, V., Vis, B., Nelson, M. & Soentken, M. (2013) 'European welfare states in motion', NEUJOBS Working Paper No.D5.2, available online at: http://www.neujobs.eu

Jessoula, M. & Vesan, P. (2011) 'Italy: limited adaptation of an atypical system', in *Regulating the Risk of Unemployment: National Adaptations to Post-industrial Labour Markets in Europe*, eds J. Clasen & D. Clegg, Oxford University Press, Oxford, pp. 142–164.

Madama, I., Natili, M. & Jessoula, M. (2013) *National Report: Italy*, COPE, available online at: http://cope-research.eu/?page_id=377

Petmesidou, M. (2013) 'Southern Europe', in *International Handbook of the Welfare State*, ed. B. Greve, Routledge, London, pp. 183–192.

Petmesidou, M. & Mossialos, E. (2006) *Social Policy Developments in Greece*, Ashgate, Aldershot.

Petmesidou, M. & Polyzoidis, P. (2013) 'Religion und Wohlfahrtsstaatlichkeit in Griechenland', in *Religion und Wohlfahrtsstaatlichkeit in Europa*, eds H.-R. Reuter & K. Gabriel, Mohr Siebeck, Stuttgart, pp. 177–214.

Pierson, P. (2011) 'Welfare state reform over the (very) long-run', Working Paper, Centre for Social Policy, University of Bremen.

Sacchi, S. & Bastagli, F. (2005) 'Italy: striving uphill but stopping halfway', in *Welfare State Reform in Southern Europe: Fighting Poverty and Social Exclusion in Italy, Spain, Portugal and Greece*, ed. M. Ferrera, Routledge, London, pp. 84–140.

# Reassessing South European Pensions after the Crisis: Evidence from Two Decades of Reforms

David Natali and Furio Stamati

*The article studies pension reforms in Greece, Italy, Portugal, and Spain between 1990 and 2013, focusing on three dimensions of change:* multi-pillarisation, *institutional* harmonisation, *and spending trends* (cost-containment/expansion). *The pension evolution of these countries is reassessed throughout the period of crisis and austerity. All countries encouraged the spread of private pensions and harmonised their fragmented public schemes. Cost containment was massive, putting future adequacy at risk. While international actors, especially the European Union, acquired a stronger role, that of organised labour declined. Spiralling between crisis and austerity, these systems changed and adapted, but still face old and new problems: inequality, risk individualisation, and increasing vulnerability to external shocks.*

Over the last years, South-European (SE) pension policies have been substantially reformed. Cost-containment measures were coupled, in some respects, with more ambitious attempts to recalibrate old-age protection. The present contribution sheds light on the reforms introduced between 1990 and 2013 and their major institutional and distributional consequences. The amount of policy change that has occurred in these countries is evaluated looking at three dimensions: the changing interplay between public and supplementary schemes (*multi-pillarisation*), the reduction in the fragmentation of the public pillar (*harmonisation*), and the overall level of public pension spending (*cost containment vs. expansion*).

After two decades of reforms, do these systems still belong to a coherent pension and welfare model? Do these countries show much variation in their reform records? Or do they still share some key institutional characteristics? To address these questions, we take stock of the political and institutional legacies of the SE pension model. Tracing its troubled evolution, between socio-economic challenges and 'external constraint', we progressively see the SE welfare regime lose some of its defining characteristics – at least in the field of pensions – while reaffirming its regional congruence as the (ill-fated) social model of a financially strained Euro-periphery.

In what follows, Section one summarises the main traits of the South European social model, looking at the main characteristics of pension systems in it and the main socio-economic challenges these systems have dealt with. Section two presents the empirical evidence from the four countries in question: Greece, Italy, Portugal, and Spain. We briefly present the main reforms introduced in recent years and the main traits of the politics of pensions. In particular, we add to the long-term perspective a focus on the most recent austerity measures introduced in the context of the so-called 'Great Recession'. The subsequent sections provide evidence of stability or change in SE pension systems. Section three focuses on policy output, while Section four deals with policy outcomes and the main distributive and institutional consequences. The concluding section wraps up the major issues in the comparative analysis, discussing the changing profile of social insurance pensions in Southern Europe.

## Social Insurance Pension Systems in Southern European Political Economies

Greece, Italy, Portugal, and Spain all belong to the SE social model. In line with the definitions of Ferrera (1996) and Katrougalos and Lazaridis (2008), when compared with the rest of Continental Europe they share some peculiarities: the prominent role of cash benefits, configuring an extreme variant of a 'transfer-centred' welfare state; a huge fragmentation of social policies; the hybridisation of the occupational roots of the model with universalistic schemes; and the particularistic appropriations of welfare resources. The latter are related to low degree of stateness and, partly as a consequence, to the spread of political clientelism, as social benefits are systematically exchanged for political support and votes.

These four defining traits of the SE social model stem, to a great extent, from the peculiar functioning and organisation of SE pensions. In the early days of their pension-policy-making – roughly dating between the end of the 1910s (Italy, Spain) and the mid-1930s (Greece, Portugal) – SE countries opted for the social insurance pension model, just like Germany and France. However, various national features common across the region – such as the fragmentation of party systems, the political cleavage between left radicals and socialist reformers, long years of autocratic rule, and a comparatively belated industrialisation – all contributed to concentrating control in the hands of the state. The predominance of public control produced (everywhere, but certainly more so in Italy and Greece) a process of incremental expansion. Incrementalism unfolded as a sequence of selective compensations among electorally relevant groups. By the early 1990s, this process had induced several 'distortions' in SE pension policies. First, public schemes provided the greatest share of individual

**Table 1** Public Pensions in South-European Countries

| Public Pension Spending and Fragmentation before the Reforms (1993) | Italy | Greece* | Spain | Portugal* | EU15 |
|---|---|---|---|---|---|
| Social Spending (% of GDP) | 25.5 | 22.3 | 23.7 | 24.3 | 29.1 |
| Pension Spending (% of Social spending) | 56 | 50 | 43 | 46 | 45 |
| First pillar fragmentation (Number of funds) | 47 (including 'substitutive regimes') | $\approx$ 100 (1$^{st}$ tier); $\approx$ 200 (2$^{nd}$ tier) | 11 ($\approx$ 100 in the 1970s) | 10 | – |

*Sources:* Eurostat; Funds data: Immergut, Anderson & Schulze 2007; ASISP 2009a; 2009b; 2009c; 2009d; Nektarios 2000.
*Note:* *Spending figures refer to 1995.

pension income through generous and widespread earnings-related benefits. Financing was usually PAYG (pay as you go), so that current contributions and tax revenues were immediately used to pay benefits (Table 1).

At the same time, pension hypertrophy also meant crowding out supplementary provisions (Table 2), imposing more demands on the public sector for pension top-ups. Political dynamics and the lack of non-public alternatives overburdened the pension policy with concessions to powerful social groups. This could only add up to the overall fragmentation of rights, rules, and providers, whose main demarcation lines were occupation, gender, and region of residence.

The political and financial prominence of social and pension insurance and the adherence to a 'male-breadwinner' model were the source of a second distortion. Workers received old-age protection directly, whereas inactive individuals were insured only as 'relatives' of the wage-earner. As a result, care responsibilities and family instability were not fully recognised as social risks, leaving poverty niches among women and the atypically employed.

**Table 2** Evolution of Private Pensions in South European Countries

| | Greece | Italy | Portugal | Spain |
|---|---|---|---|---|
| **Private Pensions Assets (1995)*** | | | | |
| Funds' assets (% of GDP) | 12.7% | 3.0% | 9.9% | 5.7% |
| **Private Pensions Assets and Coverage (2007)** | | | | |
| Funds' assets (% of GDP) | 0.0 | 3.2 | 13.2 | 8.2 |
| Coverage (% of working age population) | 0.0 | 15.7 | 8.7† | 33.5‡ |
| **Private Pensions Assets and Coverage (2012)** | | | | |
| Funds' assets (% of GDP) | 0.0 | 5.6 | 8.8 | 8.4 |
| Coverage (% of working age population) | 0.2 | 14 | 8.4 | 33.6‡ |

*Sources:* OECD 1997; 2009; 2011; 2012.
*Notes:* *Including some public pension funds and public enterprises' funds; †Data for 2009; ‡Own calculation on national and OECD data.

Finally, these systems offered redistribution: their universalistic ambitions were much higher than in Germany's 'Continental purebred'. The rules of earnings-related benefits, in fact, typically included social assistance measures for the elderly or for disadvantaged categories of workers. The latter comprised, for instance, minimum supplements (helping low wage contributors) or higher revaluation rates for the first contribution years (helping discontinuous careers). However, the resulting lack of a real separation between insurance and assistance brought about regressive redistributive patterns and a transparency deficit, fostering the impression of a chaotic and unfair pension labyrinth.

In the last decades of the twentieth century, such an unbalanced configuration of pensions revealed itself as particularly vulnerable to the challenges of population ageing and slow productivity growth (Table 3).

Starting from the economic challenges, over the period 1997–2007, both Italy and Portugal lagged behind the comparable Euro Area figure of +1.8 per cent yearly GDP (gross domestic product) growth rate. While Spain and Greece showed a more dynamic (and volatile) performance, productivity growth and public debt trends indicate the structural problems and lack of sustainability of SE economies. The yearly growth rate of labour productivity per employee was, on average, negative in Italy and almost null in Spain. Once again, productivity rose steadily in Greece (+2.4 per cent a year on average) and grew in line with the Euro Area Figure (+0.83 per cent) in Portugal (+0.87 per cent). And yet public debt grew faster than the rest of the economy in both countries: +0.53 per cent over GDP a year on average in Greece; +2.1 per cent a year in Portugal. Let us look at public debt as an indicator of economic health: in 2007 three out of four countries had a debt over GDP ratio higher than the 60 per cent Maastricht criteria, Italy and Greece totalling beyond 100 per cent. Only Spain (36.3 per cent) was, at the time, in an enviable position.

Unsurprisingly, then, the *Great Recession* hit very hard the financial sector and public debt of these countries. Average yearly GDP growth plummeted and turned deep red, ranging from −4.5 per cent a year in Greece to −1.02 per cent in Portugal (compared with a milder contraction of −0.58 points for the Euro Area). Public debt soared and grew by 4.4 (Italy) to 10.4 (Greece) percentage points a year on average. Expansion, including bank bailouts, boiled down to public debts growing by about 70 points in Greece, about 30 points in Italy between 2008 and 2013, and almost doubling and tripling, respectively, in Portugal and Spain. The emergency led to a stronger 'external constraint' and the direct intervention of the so-called Troika (International Monetary Fund [IMF], European Central Bank [ECB], and European Commission) in Greece and Portugal.

To make matters worse, Greece, Italy, Portugal, and Spain are also among the fastest-ageing societies in the EU27. Even if in 2010 their elderly dependency ratio (the population aged 65 + over that aged 20–64) was close to EU27 levels (28 per cent), forecasts for 2050 suggest a steady deterioration (slightly more than 60 per cent against 55 per cent in the EU27). Both rising life expectancy at 65 and below-replacement total fertility are among the determinants of this reversal of the population age structure.

**Table 3** Reform Pressures on South European Pension Systems

| Main Economic, Fiscal and Demographic Determinants of the SE Pension Challenge | Greece | Italy | Portugal | Spain |
|---|---|---|---|---|
| **Economic trends** | | | | |
| Average yearly GDP growth (%): 1997–2007 (2008–13) | +3.4 (−4.4) | +1.15 (−1.48) | +1.5 (−1.15) | +2.6 (−0.97) |
| Yearly labour productivity growth (%): 2001–07 (2008–13) | +2.4 (−1.03) | −0.09 (−0.96‡) | +0.87 (+0.9) | +0.01 (+2.07) |
| **Fiscal trends** | | | | |
| Public debt (%): 2013 (2007) | 175.1 (107.4) | 132.6 (103.3) | 129 (68.4) | 93.9 (36.3) |
| Yearly public debt growth (%): 2001–07 (2008–13) | +0.53 (+10.4) | −0.71 (+4.4) | +2.1 (+9.6) | −2.8 (+8.95) |
| **Demographic trends** | | | | |
| Elderly dependency (%) (2050) | 31 (63) | 33 (61) | 29 (61) | 27 (62) |
| *Total Fertility Rate (2050) | 1.52 (1.78) | 1.48 (1.80) | 1.32 (1.65) | 1.50 (1.81) |
| Life expectancy: men; *women* (at 65), 2010 | 78.3*; 83.0* (17.9; 20.2) | 79.5*; 84.9* (18.1; 21.7) | 76.8*; 82.8* (17.1; 20.4) | 78.8*; 85.2* (18.2; 22.1) |
| **Policy trends** | | | | |
| Effective exit age: men; *women* | 62.4; 62.3 | 61.4; 61.1 | 63.4; 63.7 | 62.5; 63.7 |
| Public pension expenditure and projections (%): 2011 (2050) | 14.9 (15.4) | 16.1 (15.7) | 14.8 (13.1) | 11.4 (14.0) |

*Source:* Eurostat data; CEC & SPC 2012.
*Notes:* *Data from OECD 2012; †Data only until 2012.

As a result, all of the SE countries, except for Spain (10.1 per cent), presented a higher level of pension spending than the EU27 (11.3 per cent), with a negative outlook. This financial burden, greatly magnified by the economic slowdown, will increase, notwithstanding the many reforms already undertaken.

Taking a step from this essential backdrop, we now introduce the historical comparative argument we suggest to characterise the evolution of SE pension systems. We conceive the SE welfare model as normatively deficient but, at the same time, synergic with productive systems that are best characterised as 'Mixed Market Economies' (MME) (Hancké, Rhodes & Thatcher 2007), where the state and the party system have considerable control over the economy. The progressive erosion of the political and economic sources of this power, however, calls this model into question. This ushered in a period of two decades of welfare reform and reinforced the 'external constraint' of European integration. While reforms have addressed key distortions of the SE social model, these four countries remain largely unable to solve the endemic problems of their political economies. We can conceive of pensions policy as a subsystem interacting with other subsystems (such as budgetary and micro-economic policies) within MMEs. The strength/weakness of each subsystem depends on the institutional complementarities that characterise the political economy of the country. As proved by the evidence we present below, while pension reform has been impressive and some major problems have been addressed (e.g. high spending and inequalities), other problems are still there (widespread contribution evasion; high labour costs). What is more important, the countries' economic vulnerability has persisted (and worsened since the *Great Recession*) and has thus contributed to tensions in the pension field.

## Reform Trends in Southern European Pension Systems, 1990–2013

In this Section we focus on the main reform trends of the 20 years up to 2013 (Table 4) and their political dynamics. Two main aspects of the latter are to be stressed. First, social partners have played a key but declining role. In some cases (see Italy and Greece), trade unions' opposition vetoed reform proposals thanks to their extraordinary mobilisation capabilities; while in others social concertation and bi/tripartite agreements have led to important reforms with limited social opposition. Afterwards, social partners' influence has been largely neutralised by policymakers through a process of strategic learning and the opportunistic use of emergency rescue packages; and the more stringent pressure coming from international organisations and the European Union (EU) in particular. External constraints have been a traditional feature of SE pension politics. As stressed below, Portugal and Greece have repeatedly asked for the financial assistance of the IMF and the EU since 1970s, while the run-up to European Monetary Union (EMU) was a decisive incentive to reforms in the 1990s. Yet, the more recent 'Memorandums of Understanding' signed by Greece and Portugal and the more subtle conditions imposed on Italy and Spain have been a more explicit pressure on national policymakers.

**Table 4** Main Pension Reforms in South European Countries (1990–2013)

| | Before the *Great Recession* | | Since the *Great Recession* |
|---|---|---|---|
| | 1990–99 | 2000–08 | 2009–12 |
| Greece | 1990: Souflias Reform<br>1991: Fakiolas Reform<br>1992: Sioufas Reform<br>1999: Spraos Reform | 2002: Reppas Reform<br>2008: Law 3655 | 2010: Law 3863 and Law 3865<br>2011: Law 3986<br>2012: Follow-up of the<br>Memorandum |
| Italy | 1992/93: Amato Reform<br>1995: Dini Reform<br>1997: Prodi Reform | 2004: Berlusconi Reform<br>2007: Welfare Protocol | 2009/10: Berlusconi Reforms<br>2011: Monti/Fornero Reform |
| Portugal | 1993: Decree Law 392<br>1999: Decree Law 199 | 2000: Framework Law<br>2001: Decree Law 331<br>2002: Decree Law 35<br>2002: Framework Law<br>2007: Framework Law no. 4<br>and Decree Law 187<br>2008: Reform of Disability<br>pensions | 2011: Austerity package<br>2012–13: Austerity measures |
| Spain | 1995: Toledo Pact<br>1997: Aznar Reform | 2001: Pension Pact<br>2007: Social Pact | 2011: New Toledo Pact and<br>Act 27/2011<br>2012: Royal Decree 17/2012<br>2013: Sustainability Factor Law |

*Source:* Authors' elaboration.

## Greece: Glass-Cracking in a Reform Laggard

At the beginning of the 1990s, Greek pensions were based on the public (first) pillar that provided basic and auxiliary pensions with a PAYG and defined-benefit method of financing. Social insurance funds were self-governing bodies managed by representatives of employees, employers, and the state. The system was characterised by a high degree of fragmentation and high public spending.

The early 1990s were marked by the attempt to address major policy problems. As stressed by Triantafillou (2007), in a gloomy economic context both the European institutions and the IMF asked for reform on pensions and public budgetary policy. The centre-right government acted to contain public spending, supporting macroeconomic adjustment, while preparing a more radical reform of the pension architecture. The key provisions of Law 1902/1990 and Law 2084/1992 entailed increases in contributions, introduction of contributions for civil servants, tightening of eligibility rules for disability pensions, increases in the pensionable age, and the unification of pension rights across occupational groups. In the second half of the 1990s, the centre-left Panhellenic Socialist Movement (PASOK) government further tried to increase effective retirement age, make contributions and benefits more consistent with each other, and reduce institutional fragmentation. Due to the joint opposition of trade unions and far-left parties and the lack of any bipartisan

21

consensus, only a 'mini-reform' (Law 2676/99) could pass. Path dependent and of marginal impact (Carrera, Angelaki & Carolo 2009), reforms in the decade fell short of expectations, especially as regards fostering supplementary pensions.

In the early 2000s, the same political dynamics led to further piecemeal policy changes. Following the reform failure of 2001, the PASOK government proposed the Reppas reform (Law 3029/2002). Its main innovation was the introduction of voluntary funded pension schemes to add flexibility to the system within a multi-pillar framework. Contrary to policymakers' intentions, auxiliary funds never turned into occupational schemes managed by social partners. Four occupational funds were established, but they remained of limited importance and only provided lump sum payments. Cost containment was pursued by merging schemes or harmonising retirement rules across them and by gradually reducing future benefit for civil servants.

Law 3655/2008 was a more ambitious reform. It radically reduced the number of social insurance funds from approximately 130 to 13, greatly simplifying the Greek system while improving its administrative efficiency. The reform met broad political and social support, although the trade unions remained critical of retirement age increases and stricter pension rules for arduous jobs. While institutional simplification was largely welcomed, the financial sustainability of the IKA (the Social Insurance Organisation, private employees' main scheme) raised concerns, due to the major deficits of some of its constituent schemes.

## Reforms Undertaken during the Crisis

After the economic crisis broke out in 2008/09, the Greek government agreed on a memorandum of understanding with the European Commission, the ECB, and the IMF (the so-called Troika). More radical reforms were designed to reduce public budget stress, including major cutbacks on pensions. The thirteenth and fourteenth month pension payments were abolished, and replaced by a flat-rate bonus, a tax was introduced on pensions exceeding €1,400/month, and all pensions were frozen over a three-year period (ASISP [Analytical Support on the Socio-economic Impact of Social Protection Reforms] 2010a). Following a series of amendments, the Greek Parliament approved Law 3863/2010 in July 2010 followed by further administrative measures through Law 3865/2010. Assistance and insurance functions were institutionally separated and proportionality between contributions and benefits reinforced. From 2015, pension benefits were to be made up of the newly introduced basic (flat-rate) component, and a PAYG element based on life-time earnings, which will require a 40-year employment history. While the system retained its PAYG structure, future pension benefits were estimated to be between 25 and 50 per cent lower than today's levels, in absolute cash terms. After the reform, pension spending per GDP was expected to increase by about 1.9 per cent between 2010 and 2060, while in the pre-reform scenario it was expected to grow by about 12 per cent. Further cuts were introduced following the revised Memorandum for the rescue deal of July 2011 and new ones for the second rescue deal negotiated in mid-February 2012.

In March 2012, many of the supplementary PAYG public pensions (the so-called 'auxiliary schemes') were merged into ETEA (Unified Auxiliary Pensions Fund), in line with a notional defined contribution system. The official retirement age was increased to 67 (Symeonidis 2013). While the Troika and the Memorandum led unprecedented reforms, the debt restructuring (the so called 'debt haircut') led the Greek Social Security System to lose about €8 billion. These developments put further pressures on policymakers to pass cutbacks. Administrative measures were introduced in 2013 to move further towards the merging of different pension schemes and to reduce tax evasion. In terms of pension politics the stringent new external constraint has much reduced the role of social partners and limited the room for consultation.

## Italy: Wasting the Dividend of an Early Path Shift

By the early 1990s, Italy's generous and fragmented pension system well epitomised the typical traits of the SE pension model. Economic and demographic challenges, aggravated by unfavourable activity and employment rates, cut back the long-term financial returns of PAYG financing, compromising its sustainability. With the path-breaking Amato (1992–93) and Dini (1995) reforms, the system moved towards a three-pillar structure: voluntary tax-subsidised schemes flanked a less generous and less fragmented system of public benefits and an expanded safety net. The new public system covered private and public employees, farmers, artisans, shopkeepers, and atypical 'project workers' with one same Notional Defined Contribution (NDC) scheme. Workers aged 57 to 65 could flexibly retire, receiving actuarially neutral benefits, whose value resulted from individual contribution records, revaluated in line with macroeconomic and demographic trends. Contribution rates varied from 33 per cent (private employees) to about 20 per cent (self-employed). Supplementary pensions were repeatedly reregulated until 2007, when contributions to the private sector's severance payment fund Trattamento di Fine Rapporto (Tfr) were finally made available to the new funds through 'auto-enrolment' (Natali & Stamati 2013). Supplementary schemes may take the form of 'closed pension funds' tailored to specific occupational groups; 'open pension funds' that can be freely joined, collectively or individually; and, since 2000, tax-favoured private insurance plans (PIPs) with no contributory duty for employers.

In order to obtain the cooperation of the unions, the 1995 NDC rules were implemented with extreme gradualism. Much to the discontent of the employers, the new system was applied in its entirety only to labour market entrants. Workers with at least 18 years' contribution in 1995 were fully exempted. A number of interventions have been enacted since then to harmonise the system and contain short-term costs. One of the most controversial issues has been how to phase out early retirement based on seniority. Contextually, short-term savings were realised with parametric interventions, including the abrupt increase in the age requisites for retirement legislated in 2004 (and revised in 2007).

The increasing complexity and inconsistency of the reformed system may be seen as a consequence of how Italian pension politics have evolved in the last 20 years. While a case of consensual policy change, the political logic and ambitions of the Dini reform remained unsettled. Time after time, NDC rules were thus steered closer to a different interpretation of the new pension contract, drifting away from the original deal struck by the technocrats and the centre-left.

Before the crisis, Italian pensions were thus trapped in a never-ending transition. The slow phasing in of the NDC system and the hesitant phasing out of early retirement repeatedly confronted policymakers with the need for short-term consolidation. Principally to make up for public benefit cuts, supplementary pensions suffered from limited coverage, unsatisfactory regulation, and a shortage of resources. Worsening Italy's present and future pension prospects, the crisis provided a formidable stimulus for rationalisation.

### Reforms Undertaken during the Crisis

Several austerity packages were enacted between 2009 and 2012 and policy change was substantial (ASISP 2012a). Between 2009 and 2010, Berlusconi's centre-right cabinet pursued short-term savings by tightening age requisites. In 2008 and 2010, the EU issued formal sanctions against Italy for having reintroduced gender differentials in civil servants' retirement ages. In response, Italy scheduled the gradual harmonisation of age requisites across occupations and genders by 2026. Starting in 2015, age requirements would all be aligned to life expectancy trends every three years (ASISP 2011a; 2012a).

Appointed in November 2011, Monti's caretaker government accelerated the pension transition with the Fornero reform. The unions opposed it with newfound cohesion, but their effort was marginalised by the urgency of the crisis and the resoluteness of the government. The automatic adjustment of age requirements was decided to be in force from 2021 onwards. The standard retirement age would be completely harmonised across gender and sector by 2018, reaching 67 in 2021. In order to speed up the phasing in of NDC rules, contributions paid since January 2012 were set to fall under the NDC formula, also for previously exempted workers (ASISP 2012a).

Retirement could be postponed until 70 according to a new set of divisors. The vesting period of old-age pensions in the NDC system was increased from 5 to 20 years or until the resulting pension would at least equal 1.5 times the social allowance (about €430 a month in 2012). The law also made it easier for workers with very fragmented careers to unify their contribution records. Finally, a new seniority pension in the NDC system allowed retirement up to three years before the (indexed) standard age. As an emergency measure, the indexation of benefits above €1,400 a month in 2012 and 2013 was suspended. Contribution rates for the self-employed were increased (and harmonised) to 24 per cent (Schøyen & Stamati 2013).

Overall, pension legislation in the years of the crisis was predominantly focused on cutting short- and long-term costs, in order to stabilise the public budget and regain the trust of the markets in Italian bonds. The Monti/Fornero reform, in particular, focused more decisively on rationalising the NDC system, while still acting incrementally on the existing reform path. Adequacy concerns on benefit levels were not addressed, while the focus on cost containment further worsened the pension prospects of future retirees.

### Portugal: Equalising by Levelling-off

The Portuguese pension system became a state-managed and PAYG system only in 1962. The 1976 Constitution laid the foundations for closing the system's many gaps in the direction of redistribution and universalism. However, two major fiscal crises in 1977 and 1983 – leading the Portuguese governments to ask for IMF financial aid – largely shaped the pension reform agenda in terms of cost containment (much earlier than in other SE countries) (Chulià & Asensio 2007). The Social Security Framework Law passed by the centre-right in 1984 formally distinguished contribution-financed benefits of the *Regime Geral* from (mostly) tax-financed non-contributory social assistance. Moreover, the Framework Law also provided a legislative framework for supplementary pensions. Policymakers' efforts notwithstanding, the scope of supplementary pensions in Portugal remained very limited (ASISP 2012b).

The 1990s saw new attempts to address the pension system's problems. Cost containment and the launch of supplementary pension schemes were central in the political debate. In 1993, the right-of-centre government adopted a number of parametric cuts and revisions to include newly hired civil servants in the general regime and introduced a minimum supplement (*complemento social*) up to the limit of the non-contributory 'social pension'. Back in government in 1995, the Socialists aimed to reduce financial stress on pension statutory regimes while increasing retirement age and improving the overall adequacy of the system. Following some of the recommendations of an expert Commission and a social pact with the unions, the centre-left revised the rules for early and late retirement in 1999. All this led to ambiguous reform trends: decree law 392/99 introduced new incentives for delaying retirement and for hiring older workers; while decree law 199/99 offered the long-term unemployed new opportunities to retire earlier. More generous supplements for dependent pensioners were also introduced.

The 2000s saw two major reforms. In 2000 the left-wing minority government passed the Social Security Framework Law to better divide social assistance and social protection schemes, the former financed by public budget revenues, the latter through payroll taxes. The *plafonamento* – the income ceiling above which contributions should be invested in supplementary pension funds – remained an open issue. The law was partly implemented through the preparatory work delivered by a tripartite commission (including trade unions and the employers' association). Few decrees implemented new rules of financing and cost-containment measures to reduce average replacement rates. In 2002 the right-wing government proposed a new Framework Law, encouraging the further development of supplementary pensions (*Sistema Complementar*). Opposed by trade unions and the parliamentary minority and the President of the Republic, the 2002 framework reform failed to be implemented (Chulià & Asensio 2007).

After transposing the Institutions for Occupational Retirement Provision (IORP) directive in 2006, Portugal embarked on a new pension reform. Changes in the earnings-related system were accelerated with the adoption of a pro rata system and separate mandatory schemes were closed. Full harmonisation was scheduled for 2012. The Solidarity Supplement for the Elderly, a new means-tested non-contributory benefit was implemented after 2007. A new set of state-managed supplementary funded schemes (*Certificados de reforma*) was established in 2008 (ASISP 2012b). The 2007 reform – based on agreement between the government and social partners – contained some retrenchment: the introduction of the 'sustainability coefficient', a demographic adjustment factor; benefits were to be calculated on the base of the earnings of the entire working career rather on the best years; and indexation was largely reduced (Murteira 2012).

### Reforms Undertaken during the Crisis

As the crisis aggravated Portugal's deficit and debt levels, widespread unemployment and the economic slowdown severely affected pension spending levels. From 2009, the financial crisis had already challenged the private pension schemes. In the early phase of the crisis, Portuguese funds experienced a negative return of −2.4 per cent and failed to recover in the short term, recording a loss of 10.5 per cent between December 2009 and December 2010. Pension funds' assets declined by 30 per cent from 2010 to 2011, reflecting the transfer of occupational funds in the banking sector to the Public Retirement System. Public pension spending totalled 14 per cent of GDP in 2010 (the same level previously projected for 2060) and, in December, another austerity package was announced for 2011. The government's Stability and Growth Programme (SGP) for 2011 suspended benefit indexation and led to a further cut (up to 10 per cent) on pension benefits above €1,500 per month.

Given the negative future outlook of Portuguese pensions, the Budget Law for 2012 foresaw a pension budget deficit by 2030 and an extra €150 million savings to be realised in 2012–13. The Memorandum of Understanding agreed between Portugal and the Troika in May 2011 envisioned new measures for 2011–13, such as cuts in pension indexation and pension benefit values, the strengthening of means-testing and a reduction in social expenditure of at least €350 million. Flexible retirement options were temporarily blocked for 2012. Two of the 14 monthly payments of pensions over €1,100 were suppressed for 2012 and 2013, paralleled by a gradual reduction also on benefits between €600 and €1,100. After the elections of June 2011, a centre-right government envisaged new austerity measures: an increase in the early retirement age from 55 to 57, an increase in the standard retirement age up to 67 or 68 years, new incentives for prefunding supplementary benefits, a stronger means-tested approach, and a reduction in employers' contributions. In April 2012, the government decided to suspend access to early retirement benefits. Further cutbacks were introduced between November 2012 and May 2013 (the May reform consisted of cuts of about €4.5 billion): increased taxation of benefits, further increase of the retirement age; and the revision of rules in the public sector. All these measures became an object of opposition by the trade unions and some of them were rejected by the Constitutional Court.

*Spain: Reaching a New Pension Settlement?*

From the 1960s onwards, Spanish pension spending started to catch up with European standards. The pension system comprised two main PAYG schemes. The first, contributory, scheme was mandatory for all employees and the self-employed. It followed a defined-benefit approach with redistributive elements. The second scheme, non-contributory and means tested, was introduced in 1990 to cover a minority of individuals who came short of a contributory pension. From the 1980s, supplementary pension funds were added.

The first attempts at retrenchment and recalibration, undertaken unilaterally by the Socialists, date back to 1985–87 (Guillén & Alvarez 2004). Excessive pension spending emerged as the main problem of an otherwise underdeveloped welfare state. Still, the progressive front demanded better protection for survivors and low income retirees. The Toledo Pact – drawn up by an all-party committee and endorsed by the unions and the employers – was ratified by Parliament in 1995. It struck a compromise between retrenchment and expansion. As in other SE systems, a clearer distinction between solidarity and insurance was advocated for both equity and financial reasons. Some proposals involved the creation of a reserve fund to accumulate fiscal surpluses, an increase in the retirement age, and the introduction of supplementary schemes. Others focused on fostering harmonisation, guaranteeing equality, and improving the system's administrative efficiency.

The late 1990s and early 2000s were marked by Aznar's conservative cabinet that negotiated two pacts with social partners. A first agreement, converted into law in 1997, proposed to separate different financing sources (including a reserve fund) and reinforce actuarial neutrality. Solidaristic measures ensured a broader consensus. This incremental reform had few fiscal effects. In 2001, Aznar signed another pact with the trade unions, which envisaged higher non-contributory benefits, less restrictions on early retirement, and lower employers' contributions for female and senior workers. And yet, higher employment rates, broader pension coverage, and tougher administrative controls brought financial surpluses to the system in the short term (Chuliá 2007).

After lengthy negotiations, a new social pact was signed and ratified as Law 40/2007 under the Socialist Zapatero government. The new law gradually increased pensionable earnings assessment to 15 effective years, further incentivised postponing retirement, and tightened the conditions for early retirement and disability pensions. Solidarity measures in the package comprised more generous survivors' benefits and higher minimum pension supplements. Royal Decree 1648/2007 reformed the governance of private pensions, with the aim of increasing transparency, strengthening internal control, and reregulating trans-border pensions.

To conclude, at least up until the *Great Recession*, Spanish reformers followed a balanced and consensual approach. Redistribution and cost containment proceeded in parallel, updating and strengthening the new pension mix.

### Reforms Undertaken during the Crisis

In November 2008, Prime Minister Zapatero announced a new pension reform, to be drafted by the new Toledo Pact Commission. Between December 2009 and January 2010, new recommendations were issued by the Commission with the so-called 'Sustainable Economy Strategy'. Social dialogue was applied to a general revamp of Spain's productive model and focused on a number of policies. As regards pensions, the Commission suggested a gradual increase of the standard retirement age to 67, raising to 25 years the earnings assessment period for contributory pensions, and tightening the rules for survivors' pensions and early retirement (ASISP 2010b).

An entirely new phase was opened by the strong impact of the crisis and by international pressures to protect the credibility of the Euro. While the government showed strong commitment to the National Stability Programme 2011–14, the Euro-Plus Pact was vital to unblocking the decision-making process (ASISP 2011b). In February 2011, the proposals contained in the new Toledo agreement became a major reform proposal, which was approved in August as Law 24/2011 with the acquiescence of the unions, although after difficult negotiations. The retirement age would be gradually increased from 65 to 67 years by 2022. By 2027, instead, the earnings-assessment period would be extended from 15 to 25 years, while the regulatory base to receive a standard pension increased from 35 to 37. As an incentive to remain active in the labour market, workers would enjoy an increase of two to four per cent of their base of calculation, depending on seniority. Although early or part-time retirement on a voluntary basis was nearly forbidden, individuals with at least 38.5 years of contribution could still retire at 65 with a full pension. The law also mentioned the introduction, since 2027, of a 'sustainability factor' to absorb unfavourable demographic dynamics.

Rajoy's electoral victory in November 2011 led to the speeding up of the cost-containment agenda. In 2013, pension indexation – already frozen in 2011 and limited to one per cent for 2012 (ASISP 2012c) – was capped at two per cent for pensions lower than €1,000 per month and at one per cent above this threshold. Early and partial retirement rules were tightened in July 2013. The seniority requisite for early retirement was increased to 33 years (in most cases), but individuals can only retire up to two years before the legal age (four if they are involuntarily unemployed). New rules for the sustainability factor came in December 2013, following the indications of an ad hoc expert commission. An 'intergenerational equity factor' (IEF) was planned to absorb future increases in life expectancy by reducing benefits above minimum pensions. It should take effect in 2019, eight years earlier than in the 2011 reform, and be revised every five years afterwards. A new 'annual revaluation factor' (ARF) was also introduced, keeping benefit indexation in line with trends in the pension system's budget and revenues. Future savings from the new measures are estimated at €33 billion between 2014 and 2022. Unilaterally adopted, the reform was harshly criticised by the opposition and the unions, especially for the insufficient safeguard clauses offered to jobless seniors (ASISP 2013; Pina & Gutiérrez-Domènech 2013).

Market-based provisions were not further reformed, although the government announced additional tax discounts for private pensions (January 2012). The new policy should redress the negative effects of tighter tax incentive measures adopted in 2006, tackling the issue of the comparatively low development of Spanish private pensions.

## Comparing Reforms' Outputs

As summarised by Table 4, all four countries show an impressive reform record. Policymakers in the region followed largely similar agendas: altering the pension mix, reducing institutional fragmentation, and containing public spending. And yet, timing has differed. In Italy and to some extent Spain, important reforms were passed as early as the 1990s. Greece and Portugal enacted marginal measures in the 1990s and the early 2000s, adopting a more radical approach during the *Great Recession*.

The pension mix of SE countries has changed. First, social insurance and assistance functions are more clearly distinguished across the main tiers of the first pillar: some schemes aim to provide basic protection, while others are purely earnings related. Second, benefit formulas have been revised. In line with actuarial logic, future pensions will be strictly related to individual contribution records. Italy has been the most advanced case with the shift from defined-benefit to defined-contribution PAYG schemes. In some cases, higher benefits have been curtailed through more strict calculation and higher taxation on old-age benefits. Less generous statutory schemes (should) have opened more room for supplementary funds, consistent with the spread of the multi-pillar paradigm (over the region and Europe in general). Different options have been discussed, in terms of voluntary and/or mandatory take-up. Italy partially abandoned pure voluntarism in 2004 with the introduction of 'auto-enrolment' to increase pension funds' coverage. Yet the actual development of occupational and individual pensions has been limited. This is especially the case for Greece and Portugal, where coverage and assets are both meagre. In those countries where supplementary schemes have spread the most, i.e. Italy and Spain, a major problem is the increased segmentation of pension rights across occupational and social groups (see section below).

The second common line of action has been the attempt to reduce institutional fragmentation. All the SE systems have been reformed in an attempt to increase economy of scale with a reduction of administrative costs, and to improve equality across social and occupational groups. The number of statutory pension regimes has been greatly reduced in Greece and in Italy. Such a trend has been paralleled by the increased homogeneity of rules for access to the schemes, financing and benefit setting.

Policymakers have tried to contain public spending in the context of protracted economic stagnation, low productivity and persistent unemployment, and worrying demographic projections. Cost containment has consisted of a set of measures shared by SE policymakers: increased retirement age, more limited access to early retirement, less generous indexation, strict application of means-testing for the provision of basic pensions; stricter linkage between contributions and pension benefits. New 'demographic' or sustainability factors have aimed to automatically adjust spending in accordance with demographic and economic trends. In parallel, pension systems' revenues have increased, with higher contribution rates (at least for some categories). Retrenchment has been accompanied by some increase of survivors' pension benefits (in Spain) and higher minimum pension supplements (see Portugal and Greece).

Comparing the four reform processes reveals that the path towards more sustainable pension systems is yet unfinished. Firstly, old distortions have not been fully addressed. The incongruence between performance-based and citizenship-based entitlements became too costly to sustain within a single public pillar, but remained politically untenable outside of it. Secondly, although multi-pillarisation and harmonisation could be synergic with a less generous public system, the same fiscal shortage and the old inability to choose between Beveridge and Bismarck prevented once again a clear demarcation of pension functions within these systems. So, while most work pensions are pushed to social assistance levels, private pension supplements are underdeveloped. This suggests that the SE pension model is currently assuming a new common trait: an unintentional residualism due to the more meagre first pillar protection and the failed (almost failed in Italy and Spain) spread of supplementary funds.

## Comparing Reform Outcomes

In this section we briefly review the most recent pension policy outcomes, cautiously assessing the combined impact of crisis and austerity. We focus on three dimensions: long-term financial effects, access and adequacy, and poverty and inequality (Table 5 below). It is worth noticing here that these dimensions are not related to the institutional trends of multi-pillarisation, harmonisation, and cost containment. On the contrary, they are best conceived as a result of the underlying social, structural, and historical scenario where old and new policies happen to operate.

Similarities in the four reform patterns led to similar long-term financial effects: spending stabilisation in Italy and Spain, spending reductions in Portugal and Greece. As regards access, yearly observations are lacking. Still, given knowledge of policymakers' goals, a number of considerations can be advanced. A first item is the coverage of targeted (means-tested) and minimum pensions. Targeted benefits cover slightly less than 20 per cent of the elderly population, with the exception of Italy (5 per cent); slightly more than 30 per cent receive instead a minimum pension, excluding Greece (60 per cent). These figures become alarming considering how heavily minimum supplements have been reformed in SE systems. Reducing or

**Table 5** Outcomes of the Reforms

| | Greece | Italy | Portugal | Spain |
|---|---|---|---|---|
| **Long-term financial effects** | | | | |
| Public pension 2050 spending forecasts (%): 2006–12 change (2006 projections) | −8.6* (24)* | +1.1 (14.6) | −7.7 (20.8) | −1.7 (15.7) |
| **Access and Adequacy** | | | | |
| Percentage of 65 + population receiving targeted (minimum) pensions (%) | 19 (60) | 5 (32) | 17.4 (33.8) | 19.6 (33.9) |
| Theoretical net replacement rates (42 years' contribution, average wage): | 126.1% | 89.3% | 103.8% | 98.2% |
| 2010 (2050–2010 change) | (−37.2 p.p.)‡ | (−13.7 p.p.) | (−21.6 p.p.) | (−5.9 p.p.) |
| Aggregate replacement rate (%): men; *women* | 48; *44* | 58; *44* | 57; *55* | 61; *47* |
| **Poverty and Inequality** | | | | |
| At-risk-of-poverty (severe deprivation) (%): 65 − ; *65 +* | 19.9 (11.4); | 18.6 (7.1); | 17.2 (10.9); | 20.5 (4.4); |
| | *21.3 (12.4)* | *16.6 (6.2)* | *21 (9.6)* | *21.7 (2)* |
| Gini index in 2010 (2007): pensions; *wages* | 16.2 (29.7†); | 23.4 (22.8); | 29.1 (28.9†); | 19.8 (25.8); |
| | *27.1 (30.6†)* | *23.8 (23.1)* | *29.4 (33.5†)* | *26.2 (30.8)* |

*Sources:* CEC 2006; CEC & SPC 2012; OECD 2012.
*Notes:* *2012–2009 change (2006 projections not available); †Data for 2011 (2007–09 data not available); ‡p.p. = percentage points.

eliminating them is likely to put greater (and possibly unforeseen) pressure on targeted benefits, which would then start paying more than half of the national pension bill.

When we look at adequacy, current net replacement rates after a theoretically continuous career of 42 years are close to or above 100 per cent of individual last wage. Here, Italy is the exception, as the reforms of the 1990s have already started to downsize benefits. Once again, foreseen reductions will bring these figures well below 100 per cent by 2050, concentrating the negative impact of the reforms on younger generations (even for individuals with exceptionally long/continuous careers). Aggregate replacement rates show, however, how much the theoretical figures overestimate the average retiree's life conditions. In all four countries, but especially in Italy and Spain, an overall gender gap exists, pushing female pensioners close to or below the poverty threshold.

Coverage data for private pensions, already shown in Table 2, suggest that the transition to a fully fledged multi-pillar architecture is far from complete in Italy and Spain, hung up in Portugal, and never started in Greece. Data on assets in Figure 1 confirm this analysis from a different perspective: that of the stock of assets accumulated in the private pillars. Moreover, wherever disaggregated figures exist, they suggest strong and increasing inequality in access to supplementary pensions (see Natali and Stamati [2013] on Italy, and ASISP [2012c] on Spain).

To conclude with poverty and inequality, in SE the elderly are commonly more exposed to the risk of poverty than the rest of the population (Italy being the exception). At the same time, excluding Greece, basic social assistance makes them less exposed to the risk of severe material deprivation (especially so in Spain). On the

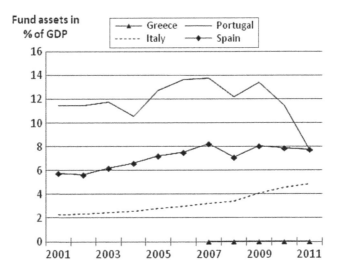

**Figure 1** Trends in Pension Fund Assets in SE Countries (% of GDP, 2001–11). *Source:* OECD 2012.

bright side, Portugal is the only case where the poverty gap disfavouring the elderly is above two per cent. Measuring inequality through the Gini index, Italy and Portugal appear more loyal to the Bismarckian non-redistributive blueprint, whereas pension income in Greece and Spain is substantially less concentrated than wages. From an inter-temporal perspective, one could ask whether crisis and austerity have increased inequality or compressed both pensions and wages down the income scale. Data show that, between 2007 and 2010, the second scenario has been the rule, especially for Greek and Spanish pensioners. However, this was not the case in Italy and for Portuguese retirees, where the picture is rather one of stability.

## Conclusions

South European pension systems have been largely reformed in the last two decades. Problem pressures, long-term deficiencies, and external constraints have all contributed to put pensions on the agenda. Reforms have been consistent with three main policy measures: the revision of the pension mix in line with the multi-pillar paradigm; the progressive harmonisation of rules with the reduction of institutional fragmentation (especially across occupational groups); and cost containment.

The reforms have altered some key traits of the SE model in all these respects. High pension spending has been addressed through a broad set of cost-containment measures: higher retirement age, less generous indexation, and the introduction of demographic factors linking benefits to adverse demographic trends. Public pension rules have been harmonised and most privileges cut, while the number of public schemes has been lowered through merging. The aim to reduce institutional fragmentation has limited inequalities and inefficiencies in the first pillar. Cost containment has been massive (especially in the context of the *Great Recession*), with expected future negative effects on the adequacy of pension benefits. And all the countries have supported the launch and spread of supplementary pension funds.

The politics of pension reform has also been marked by change. The role of external constraints has become increasingly evident. While EU and international organisations have played a role since the 1970s, their pressure has increased, reaching its apex in the case of the most recent economic crisis. The EU resorted to a number of instruments: economic and budgetary coordination, legislation on occupational pensions, rulings of the European Court of Justice, as well as a new form of conditionality. This has been paralleled by the decline of trade unions and their capacity to shape reforms.

Yet reforms' output and outcomes prove the mixed success of the process and the differences between countries. The public monopoly of old-age insurance has been weakened, but the multi-pillar model is far from accomplished, as the reduction of public pensions failed to automatically crowd in private supplements. The latter still play a minor role in Greece and Portugal and have added a new source of social segmentation of pension rights in Italy and Spain, where their weight is more substantial. If the problem pressure of the crisis and the political pressures of the EU level have indeed brought about reforms that were previously considered both unpopular and unlikely, they look far less conducive to changes that may be both resolving and legitimate.

While the SE pension model has lost some of its defining features, it is now kept together by its persistent vulnerability to external shocks. On the one hand, the massive cutbacks have reduced risks for the long-term sustainability of the system but they have not led to the solution of major challenges (high level of labour costs, increased taxation, huge tax and contribution evasion). On the other, weak economic performance and persistent budgetary tensions risk putting the whole welfare system under increased pressure. And, while the declining role of social partners and especially trade unions seems to lead to an easier reform process, it is a source of challenge for instance in the development of supplementary pensions (occupation second pillar). As a result, SE public benefits are increasingly pushed towards social assistance levels by a sluggish economy, the fiscal frailty of their budgets, and the hardness of the external constraint. In turn, supplementary provisions will need presently unattainable levels of confidence, social dialogue, and tax discounts.

In sum, SE pension systems may end up with the worst of both the Bismarckian and the Beveridgean worlds: an unprecedented model where earnings-related schemes are complemented by increasing residualism at the bottom and risk individualisation (with corporatist influences) at the top. All this proves that pension reforms have only partly contributed to a sound and coherent recasting of the 'Mixed' political economies of Southern Europe. The needed complementarity between subsystems – budgetary policy, public social insurance, industrial relations, and occupational welfare – is still missing. Only the next iterations of an ongoing reform process will tell whether this vulnerability will be the premise of the system's rejuvenation or the prelude to its demise.

## Acknowledgements

The authors wish to thank the editors of the special issue, as well as the journal's editors and the anonymous referees, for comments.

## References

ASISP. (2009a) 'Annual Report 2009 - Greece', available online at: http://socialprotection.eu/
ASISP. (2009b) 'Annual Report 2009 - Italy', available online at: http://socialprotection.eu/
ASISP. (2009c) 'Annual Report 2009 - Portugal', available online at: http://socialprotection.eu/
ASISP. (2009d) 'Annual Report 2009 - Spain', available online at: http://socialprotection.eu/
ASISP. (2010a) 'Annual Report 2010 - Greece', available online at: http://socialprotection.eu/
ASISP. (2010b) 'Annual Report 2010 - Spain', available online at: http://socialprotection.eu/
ASISP. (2011a) 'Annual Report 2011 - Italy', available online at: http://socialprotection.eu/
ASISP. (2011b) 'Annual Report 2011 - Spain', available online at: http://socialprotection.eu/
ASISP. (2012a) 'Annual Report 2012 - Italy', available online at: http://socialprotection.eu/
ASISP. (2012b) 'Annual Report 2012 - Portugal', available online at: http://socialprotection.eu/
ASISP. (2012c) 'Annual Report 2012 - Spain', available online at: http://socialprotection.eu/

ASISP. (2013) 'Annual Report 2013 - Spain', available online at: http://socialprotection.eu/

Carrera, L. N., Angelaki, M. & Carolo, D. (2010) 'Political competition and societal veto players. The politics of pension reforms in Southern Europe', *Rivista Italiana di Politiche Pubbliche*, vol. 2010, no. 1, pp. 5–31.

CEC. (2006) *The Long-term Sustainability of Public Finances in the European Union*, European Economy, no. 4, 'European Commission', available online at: http://ec.europa.eu/economy_finance/publications/publication7903_en.pdf

CEC & SPC. (2012) *Pension Adequacy in the European Union 2010–2050*, POEU, Luxembourg.

Chulià, E. (2007) 'Spain: between majority rule and incrementalism', in *The Handbook of West European Pension Politics*, eds E. M. Immergut, K. M. Anderson & I. Schulze, Oxford University Press, Oxford, pp. 499–554.

Chulià, E. & Asensio, M. (2007) 'Portugal: in search of a stable framework', in *The Handbook of West European Pension Politics*, eds E. M. Immergut, K. M. Anderson & I. Schulze, Oxford University Press, Oxford, pp. 605–669.

Ferrera, M. (1996) 'The southern model of welfare in social Europe', *Journal of European Social Policy*, vol. 6, no. 1, pp. 17–37.

Guillén, A. M. & Álvarez, S. (2004) 'The EU's impact on the Spanish welfare state: the role of cognitive Europeanization', *Journal of European Social Policy*, vol. 14, nos. 3, pp. 285–299.

Hancké, B., Rhodes, M. & Thatcher, M. (eds) (2007) *Beyond Varieties of Capitalism: Conflict, Contradiction,and Complementarities in the European Economy*, Oxford University Press, Oxford.

Immergut, E. M., Anderson, K. M. & Schulze, I. (eds) (2007) *The handbook of West European Pension Politics*, Oxford University Press, Oxford.

Katrougalos, G. & Lazaridis, G. (2008) 'The South European welfare states at the dawn of the new millennium: identity and problems', *Social Cohesion and Development*, vol. 3, no. 1, pp. 5–25.

Murteira, M. C. (2012) 'The reform of rensions in Portugal: a critical assessment', in *Old Age Crisis and Pension Reforms. Where Do We Stand?* ed. M. Szczepansky, Publishing House of Poznan University of Technology, Poznan.

Natali, D. & Stamati, F. (2013) 'Le pensioni "categoriali" in Italia: legislazione e messa in opera del nuovo sistema multi-pilastro', in *Tempi Moderni. Il Welfare nelle aziende in Italia*, eds E. Pavolini, U. Ascoli & M. L. Mirabile, Il Mulino, Bologna, pp. 83–114.

Nektarios, M. (2000) 'Financing public pensions in Greece', *SPOUDAI*, vol. 50, nos. 3–4, pp. 125–139.

OECD. (1997) *Ageing Populations and the Role of the Financial System in the Provision of Retirement Income in the OECD Area*, OECD, Paris.

OECD. (2009) *Pensions at a Glance 2009: Retirement-Income Systems in OECD Countries*, OECD, Paris.

OECD. (2011) *Pension Markets in Focus*, OECD, Paris.

OECD. (2012) *Pensions Outlook*, OECD, Paris.

Pina, J. D. & Gutiérrez-Domènech, M. (2013) 'Pension reform in Spain: necessary . . . but sufficient?', in *Dossier: The Challenges of the Pension System, Monthly Report 11, Economic and Financial Market Outlook*, no 373, November, ed. la Caixa Research, la Caixa, Barcelona.

Schøyen, M. A. & Stamati, F. (2013) 'The political sustainability of the NDC pension model. The cases of Sweden and Italy', *European Journal of Social Security*, vol. 15, no. 1, pp. 79–101.

Symeonidis, G. (2013) 'The Greek pension reform strategy 2010–2013. Steering away from the tip or the iceberg?', paper presented at the World Pension Summit, 13–14 November, Amsterdam.

Triantafillou, P. (2007) 'Greece: political competition in a majoritarian system', in *The Handbook of West European Pension Politics*, eds E. M. Immergut, K. M. Anderson & I. Schulze, Oxford University Press, Oxford, pp. 605–669.

# South European Healthcare Systems under Harsh Austerity: A Progress– Regression Mix?

Maria Petmesidou, Emmanuele Pavolini and Ana M. Guillén

*This article addresses the question of whether the economic crisis provides a politically opportune time to drastically curtail public healthcare in South Europe or whether, instead, there are signs of longer-term reform strategies for potentially balancing fiscal targets with the quest for enhanced value and health outcomes, when eventually growth resumes. After a brief examination of the profile of healthcare systems in Greece, Italy, Portugal and Spain prior to the crisis, we comparatively assess the mix of retrenchment, restructuring and recalibration strategies. The effects of the austerity-driven reforms on current (and expected) health outcomes are also briefly analysed. We conclude with reflections on the future of public healthcare in South Europe.*

This article examines healthcare reform in Southern Europe (SE) under the impact of the economic crisis and austerity. Specifically, it examines the cases of Greece, Italy, Portugal and Spain. By drawing upon the available literature on welfare state retrenchment (Pierson 1994; Hacker 2004; Streeck & Thelen 2005), we raise the following questions: What 'recalibration' strategies (if any) are underway? Is retrenchment (and any scaling back of public provision) a conjunctural effect of the fiscal woes SE countries are facing? Is there any evidence of 'policy drift' causing parts of public provision to wither away? How likely is a large-scale, permanent retreat of the state from the health sector? Undoubtedly a long time span is required to thoroughly assess the transformative (or non-transformative) effects of reform. However, as the crisis has increased the urgency and political priority of the healthcare issue in all four countries, there is enough evidence to trace fundamental levers of reform, and come up with a preliminary assessment of the direction and degree of change.

We start with a brief overview of the healthcare systems in the four countries in the years preceding the crisis. We trace their diverse paths and common concerns, their achievements and major predicaments. The second part examines the magnitude of fiscal constraint in healthcare and the third assesses the policy tools deployed in the two 'bailout' countries (Greece and Portugal) in comparison with Spain and Italy, which are also experiencing an intense crisis. In part four we trace the impact of austerity-driven reforms on current and expected health outcomes. The paper concludes with reflections on the future of SE healthcare systems.

## How Did SE Healthcare Systems Fare before the Crisis?

All four countries introduced a universal health system in the late 1970s to early 1980s. Yet transition from health insurance to a national health service (NHS) took place at a different pace and involved a varying scope of coverage in each country (Guillén 2002; Petmesidou & Guillén 2008; Petmesidou 2013a). Particularly in Greece (but also in Portugal), such a transition did not reach the state of a fully fledged NHS, as in both countries healthcare remained fragmented (Davaki & Mossialos 2006; Barros, Machado & de Almeida Simões 2011). Spain and Italy succeeded in forming more 'progressive' public healthcare systems along universalist principles. Moreover, in the latter countries a thorough transformation from a centralised to a regionalised system accompanied the introduction of the NHS (Pavolini & Guillén 2013).

In Greece, until recently, a mixed system continued to operate in terms of both funding and provision: an occupation-based health insurance system was combined with an NHS, but private provision was also expanding until the eve of the crisis. Equally, in Portugal, the NHS, established in 1979 as a universal and largely tax-financed system, has been complemented by special public and private insurance schemes ('health insurance subsystems') that cover about one-quarter of the population (mainly civil servants but also some private sector employees). A regional administrative reorganisation was first introduced in 1993, but further reform took place in 2003, in the context of a comprehensive overhaul separating regulation, financing and provision. In Greece regional health authorities were established in the early 2000s, but this hardly set up a new model for system financing and governance until recently.

In all four countries, total health expenditure stood at about nine to ten per cent of gross domestic product (GDP) for much of the second half of the 2000s. In 2010 private spending was highest in Greece (about four per cent of GDP), followed by Portugal (three per cent), and lowest in Italy and Spain (about two per cent). In all SE countries, private health spending consists of out-of-pocket payments, while private health insurance is negligible (in 2008 it ranged between one and eight per cent of total health expenditure [Table 1]).

**Table 1** Annual Average Change Rate and Percentage Constitution of Health Expenditure

| | Annual average change rate in real terms, 2000–08* | | | Percentage constitution of total health expenditure (2008/12) | | |
|---|---|---|---|---|---|---|
| | Total health expenditure | Public health expenditure | Pharmaceutical expenditure* | Public | Private (out-of-pocket) | Private insurance |
| Greece | +6.9 | +6.9 | +9.9 | 65/68 | 34/30 | 1/2 |
| Italy | +2.3 | +3.4 | −0.8 | 79/78 | 20/20 | 1/2 |
| Portugal | +2.2 | +2.0 | +2.3 | 65/63 | 27/32 | 8/5 |
| Spain | +6.0 | +6.2 | +1.5 | 73/74 | 20/20 | 7/6 |
| EU-15 | +3.7 | +3.8 | – | – | – | – |

Source: OECD health statistics, available online at: http://www.oecd-ilibrary.org/social-issues-migration-health/data/oecd-health-statistics_health-data-en; and WHO health statistics, available online at: http://apps.who.int/gho/data/
Note: *For pharmaceutical expenditure, 2000–09.

From 2000 to 2008, in Greece and Spain, healthcare spending expanded rapidly: growth in both total and public expenditure was twice that registered in the European Union (EU)-15, whereas Italy and Portugal increased their expenditure at a slower pace than the rest of Western Europe.

If we look at the amount of expenditure rather than at growth rates, the picture changes. In the second half of the 2000s, total health expenditure per capita (in Purchasing Power Parities [PPP]) was close to the EU-27 average in all four SE countries (Organisation for Economic Cooperation and Development [OECD] 2012, p. 121). However per capita public expenditure lagged behind, particularly if compared with EU-15: Italy and Spain spent around 83–85 per cent of the EU-15 per capita average, whereas Portugal and Greece spent around 65 per cent. Overall, before the crisis, an expansionary trend is evident, but differences in terms of the extent of financial control of health activity by the public sector distinguished Italy and Spain from Greece and Portugal.

This distinction is also reflected in organisational structures. In contrast to Italy and Spain, Greece and Portugal have not proceeded towards a vertically integrated system. Primary and specialist care have persistently been marked by a mixed system of service delivery by public health insurance and private providers. Primary care coverage through the NHS health centres is higher in Portugal than in Greece, but a referral system remained weak in both countries. Even though the density of doctors is comparatively high, there are claims of doctor shortages particularly in general practice and also with respect to geographic distribution in these two countries.

On the eve of the crisis, citizens' assessment of healthcare services outlined their major predicaments. Italy joins Greece and Portugal on account of the low ratings given by citizens to the quality, accessibility and affordability of hospital care and services provided by medical specialists. In the latter two countries, the lowest ratings were also given for primary care (Table 2). Spain stands out because of the comparatively positive assessment expressed by citizens for the whole range of

**Table 2** Citizens' Assessment of Healthcare Services (per cent)

| | Hospital services (2007) | | | Medical specialists (2007) | | | Primary care (2007) | | | Overall quality (bad/good) 2013 |
|---|---|---|---|---|---|---|---|---|---|---|
| | Quality (bad and fairly bad) | Access (not easy) | Not afford-able | Quality (bad and fairly bad) | Access (not easy) | Not afford-able | Quality (bad and fairly bad) | Access (not easy) | Not afford-able | |
| Spain | 18 | 16 | 10 | 19 | 28 | 22 | 11 | 6 | 7 | 22/77 |
| Italy | 37 | 31 | 33 | 25 | 39 | 49 | 23 | 17 | 16 | 42/56 |
| Portugal | 42 | 34 | 40 | 41 | 53 | 78 | 38 | 33 | 37 | 44/55 |
| Greece | 52 | 30 | 45 | 30 | 34 | 71 | 27 | 22 | 43 | 74/26 |
| EU-27 | 29 | 24 | 21 | 26 | 38 | 35 | 16 | 12 | 11 | 27/71* |

*Source:* Eurobarometer data for 2007 and 2013, available online at: http://ec.europa.eu/public_ opinion/archives/ebs/ebs_283_en.pdf; http://ec.europa.eu/ health/patient_safety/eurobarometers/ebs_411_en.htm
*Note:* *EU-28.

dimensions examined (even compared with the EU-27 average scores). Indicatively, in Greece and Portugal about two-thirds of citizens considered the services of medical and/or surgical specialists unaffordable and between a third and a half expressed a similar concern regarding primary and secondary care. When the crisis hit these countries, at least in three of them (Portugal, Greece and Italy), seriously exacerbated NHS fiscal sustainability problems were added to dissatisfaction problems of quality, access and affordability. In Portugal, and particularly in Greece, defective integration among the different parts of the system further intensified strains. Fiscal retrenchment and cost rationalisation became key priorities and, for the bailout countries, major stipulations of the rescue deals signed with the international lenders.

Strikingly, a survey conducted in late 2013 recorded a similar pattern of people's opinions on the overall quality of healthcare in the four countries. Greece stands out with a record high level of dissatisfaction (74 per cent of the respondents). In Portugal and Italy, a considerable percentage of respondents expressed negative opinions (44 and 42 per cent, respectively), while in Spain a positive view remained prevalent (77 per cent of the respondents).

## Healthcare Spending in the Crisis

Contraction measures across countries and healthcare sectors range from freezes to severe cuts. Table 3 shows the yearly average contraction rate of public health expenditure (in real terms) in the period 2009–12, and per capita public expenditure before the crisis, at its beginning and in 2012. In Greece, the crisis triggered a dramatic average annual contraction (− 11.8 per cent). Portugal and Spain followed with yearly rates of − 7.9 per cent and − 4.3 per cent respectively, whereas in Italy annual contraction was more limited (− 2.4 per cent).

The average annual contraction rate has been steepest in Greece, followed by Portugal. Per capita public health spending (in US$ PPP, at constant 2005 prices)

**Table 3** Public Expenditure Trends

| | Average annual change rate of per capita public health expenditure, in real terms (NCU at 2005 CPI rates)* | Per capita public expenditure on health (US$ purchasing power parity, at constant 2005 prices) | | |
|---|---|---|---|---|
| | 2009–12 | 2000 | 2009 | 2012 |
| Greece | − 11.8 | 949 | 1779 | 1316 |
| Italy | − 2.4** | 1562 | 1957 | 1842** |
| Portugal | − 7.9 | 1255 | 1488 | 1248 |
| Spain | − 4.3*** | 1255 | 1864 | 1791*** |
| EU-15 | − | 1720 | 2414 | 2354*** |

*Source:* OECD health statistics, as in Table 1.
*Notes:* *Own calculations on the basis of National Currency Units (NCU) at 2005 Consumer Price Index (CPI) level; **2013 data; ***2011 data.

increased from 2000 to 2009 but fell afterwards. Thus a bell curve is evident for all countries. In Greece and Portugal, contraction will continue through 2014 according to the Memoranda of Understanding (MoUs) signed with the bailout lenders. In Portugal, total public health expenditure fell from €11.6 billion in 2011 to €8.3 billion in 2013 at current prices. In Greece, public health funding stood at about €16 billion in 2009. About a third of it was slashed in the following three years and a further estimated €1.2 billion will be eliminated during 2013–14 (mostly cuts in medication spending). The overarching objective is to keep public health spending at or below six per cent of GDP – which itself has contracted by a quarter since the onset of the crisis.

In Italy, the real problem is the crucial regional variation in the quantity and quality of the services provided, to the point that national averages are misleading. Italian healthcare policy-making over the last decade has been overtly concerned with cost containment but also with the inefficient management and the corrupt practices of healthcare systems in most Southern regions. The decline of public health spending was forecast to intensify in 2014: the 2011 'Finance Bill', the main national law regulating the amount of resources allocated to the public sector, for the years 2012–14 introduced cuts equal to around €8 billion (in 2012 the overall state financing of the NHS stood at around €108 billion). However, these cuts have been 'frozen' by the 2013 'Finance Bill' and it is not clear what will happen.

In Spain, the reduction was moderate up to 2011 but then intensified: from 2009 to 2014 it has been estimated by the present government to amount to €11 billion (*El Economista* 2013, citing the Budget Plan for 2014 and 2015 sent to Brussels by the Spanish government). In 2009 the global budget of the Spanish NHS amounted to €70.3 billion; hence, a reduction of €11 billion would mean a – far from negligible – 15.6 per cent cut. The government claims, though, that a substantial part of such a cut has been carried out through savings in pharmaceutical spending.

Private expenditure has hardly substituted for the lost public spending. Between 2008–09 and 2012 out-of-pocket per capita expenditure (at constant 2005 prices) sharply decreased in Greece and contracted slightly in Italy. In Portugal and Spain, it fell in the early years of the crisis, but increased between 2009 and 2011/12 (Table 4).

Drawing upon the national household expenditure survey data for Greece, Italy and Spain, some findings stand out as particularly important with respect to inequalities in meeting healthcare needs. In Greece, from 2008 to 2012, the mean equivalised private health expenditure (at 2009 constant prices) was halved among households in the bottom and middle of the income hierarchy (that is, in the lower six income deciles). It dropped by about 30 to 40 per cent in households belonging to the seventh, eighth and ninth income deciles, but slightly increased in the top tenth income decile. In 2012, the mean equivalised private health expenditure, at current prices, ranged from €207 in the bottom decile to about €500 in the fifth and sixth income deciles, and to €2,500 in the top tenth decile) (Petmesidou et al. 2014). Given the drastic rolling back of public health expenditure, these findings indicate a deepening gap between the bottom/middle income groups and those at the top of the income hierarchy, with respect to covering medical needs.

**Table 4** Out-of-Pocket per Capita Expenditure over Time (US$ PPP at Constant 2005 Prices)

|          | 2003  | 2008   | 2009  | 2012    |
|----------|-------|--------|-------|---------|
| Greece   | n.g.  | 1010.2 | 781.5 | 557.1   |
| Italy    | 487.4 | 467.0  | 444.6 | 436.0*  |
| Portugal | 478.8 | 609.1  | 601.7 | 630.8   |
| Spain    | 493.9 | 509.8  | 488.3 | 517.8** |
| EU-15    | –     | 531.2  | 509.0 | 508.3** |

*Source*: As in Table 1.
*Notes*: *2013; **2011.

In Italy mean private health spending contracted by 11.7 per cent between 2007 and 2012.[1] Cuts in private expenditure were made by all categories of households. They were particularly harsh among households where the head is self-employed (− 23.3 per cent) or a manual worker (− 21.3 per cent). Moreover, pensioners' households were the only type of households where the expenditure on drugs slightly increased (+ 1.7 per cent), probably due to the introduction of new co-payments for medical goods that are essential for the sick elderly.

Equally, in Spain, between 2008 and 2011, the drop in average household expenditure on health was steeper among households in the lowest income bracket, with (regular) monthly household income of up to €990 net (yearly average drop − 8.8 per cent), as well as among households in the middle of the income hierarchy with a monthly income of €2,000–2,999 (− 2.4 per cent) (data from Instituto Nacional de Estadística [INE] 2011). For the higher income groups also a decrease has been observed since the outbreak of the crisis. Furthermore, the last FOESSA-Cáritas report (Fundación Fomento de Estudios Sociales y Sociología Aplicada [FOESSA] 2014) notes that, given the staggering growth in absolute poverty and social exclusion, the number of households that cannot afford to buy drugs has tripled since 2007.

In short, the crisis triggered a very drastic rolling back of public spending in Greece, a sharp decline in Portugal, a noticeable contraction in Spain and a moderate one in Italy (although in the latter country retrenchment will intensify in the coming years if the government goes ahead with the planned cuts). Notably, in all four countries, an adverse trend is varyingly manifest. As the state reduces its overall financial responsibility in healthcare, a substantial part of the cost is shifted to households and individuals. However, the crisis has also greatly squeezed private health spending. Low to middle income groups have disproportionally been hit by these conditions, which greatly limit the coverage of medical needs with serious effects on health outcome, as we show below.

## Major Reform Targets and Policies

South European healthcare systems share common challenges with other European countries regarding rising age-related expenditure, changing patterns of demands and escalating costs of medical technology. However, the prolonged recession and varying institutional predicaments in the four countries have gravely intensified fiscal strains.

In Greece and Portugal healthcare reform is a major bailout demand. In both countries financial problems were compounded by soaring hospital deficits, major cost inefficiencies and persistent fragmentation in coverage. The reform targets are framed politically as a top-down decision (and a requirement for the lenders to release the agreed bailout tranches). An overambitious language characterises the bailout agreements and the successive revision documents. The set targets range from very detailed measures concerning, among other things, budgetary and staffing cuts, hospital closures, system governance and price regulation of pharmaceutical markets, to rather vague objectives, such as modernising healthcare.

Fiscal sustainability is paramount. In both countries (and particularly so in Greece), rapid (and deep) retrenchment in public health spending, accompanied by reorganisation measures towards higher system integration, is presented as an attempt to turn efficiency gains into a stronger universalism. Yet, policy options exhibit opposite directions. For instance, reining in drug expenditure through e-prescribing and e-diagnosis systems, in parallel with the development of clinical protocols and new pricing rules for pharmaceuticals may increase efficiency savings. At the same time, however, measures are deployed that shift the cost of care away from the state (diminishing the range of service coverage, public health sector downsizing and rapidly increasing user charges [Petmesidou 2013b]). Also, staffing cuts as well as drastic reductions in health personnel salaries (and of overtime work, the volume and the price of which have been targeted for a significant reduction) greatly strain workforce capacity in such a way as may lead to seriously sacrificing quality (or even safety). Hence the question that arises for the bailout countries is how far the changes under way signpost a 'silent' shift towards a universalism of basic provisions. As shown below, increasing uncovered medical needs among the lower and middle income groups is an undisputable sign of such a turn.

In Italy and Spain, the necessity for cost containment and the search for efficiency have almost monopolised the debate on healthcare reform. This comes not only from the need to improve the economic performance of the NHS, but also (and mainly) from the need to face a huge public debt in the Italian case and a prominent (and rapidly growing) one in the case of Spain. The measures adopted are similar to those introduced in Portugal and Greece. They involve higher user charges (only for pharmaceuticals in the Spanish case); measures to control drug expenditure (higher competition in the pharmaceutical distribution market, and automatic payback systems and expenditure caps in the NHS); cuts in spending on healthcare-related goods and services (including contracted-out ambulatory and diagnostic services); hospital restructuring and downsizing. Health personnel salaries were frozen in Italy and reduced in Spain. In this latter country a clear shift towards private management of public healthcare institutions is being introduced in several regions. A central question is whether the changes imply incremental adjustment and fiscal fine-tuning, or more thorough restructuring. And in a longer-term perspective, if changes do not directly involve wholesale restructuring (privatisation), to what extent do large-scale cutbacks in public health spending and deteriorating provision indicate a kind of 'policy drift' and/or exhaustion whereby the publicly operating system gradually withers away?

## Policy Options and Tools

*Shifting the cost to patients.* In Spain the only user charge in place concerns over-the-counter pharmaceuticals (introduced in the 1970s). In 2012 co-payments were raised (from 40 per cent to a maximum of 60 per cent) for people within active ages and tuned to income level. Pensioners, traditionally exempted from user charges on drugs, now have to pay ten per cent of the cost of over-the-counter pharmaceuticals, with a maximum of €8 per month if their annual income is below €18,000. The only significant cut in service provision that has lately been introduced affects illegal immigrants: free access has been limited to pregnancy and emergency care (with the exception of irregular immigrants under 18 years of age).

In the other three countries fees and co-payments were enacted in previous decades. Recently the rates of existing user charges have increased and, in the bailout countries, new charges have been introduced. In parallel, exemptions from user charges for specific groups were partially or fully lifted (e.g. for the chronically ill, exemptions are strictly related to their chronic illness even though some of their ailments may be an indirect consequence of their health condition). Caps on laboratory tests and limits to service provision were also introduced.[2] Tax rebates for private health expenditure were abolished in Greece and significantly reduced in Portugal. In the latter country, the so-called 'moderating fees' for a visit to a primary care centre as well as 'fees' for using emergency services doubled in 2012. Co-payments for drugs increased and a charge for nurse consultation was introduced, while at the same time a 'global cap' to user charges paid per single episode of treatment was set at €50 (Barros 2012).

In Greece, since 2009 legal reforms have stipulated the all-day operation of hospitals and health centres and the charging of fees per visit in the afternoon shift to outpatients (only partly covered by social insurance). Also, an entrance fee for all (regular) outpatient services was introduced in 2010 and was raised in January 2011. In addition a 15 per cent co-payment for clinical tests was introduced for all insurees in EOPYY (Εθνικός Οργανισμός Παροχής Υπηρεσιών Υγείας – National Organisation for Health Services Provision), as well as a charge ranging from 15 to 50 per cent for different groups of EOPYY insurees for treatment in private clinics. From January 2014, on top of the existing 25 per cent user charges for pharmaceuticals, €1 per prescription has been added. A fee of €25 for every hospital admission legislated under the MoU to be in force from January 2014 was scrapped after public outcry and political pressures, even from within the governing coalition.

Moreover, an upper limit of visits per month to doctors (mostly pathologists) contracted by EOPYY, for which doctors can be reimbursed, has been in force in the last couple of years. If this limit is surpassed, then a charge of €10 to €20 is claimed from the patient. In early 2014 the ceiling was raised from 200 to 400 visits monthly (it went down to 200 in mid-2014). This took place as a response by the government to the protracted strike by medical and administrative personnel of EOPYY's health units in early 2014, because of the then pending legal reform of primary healthcare. New legislation passed in February 2014 stipulates the split between the insurance-purchasing functions (to be retained by EOPYY), and primary care provision to be undertaken by a new organisation, PEDY (Πρωτοβάθμιο Εθνικό Δίκτυο Υγείας – National Primary Healthcare Network). So far the reform has led to the downsizing of ex-EOPYY health centres, as only about half the medical personnel employed in them agreed to join PEDY as full-time public sector employees. Admittedly the reform intends to increase private provision in a mixed system embracing the 200 or so rural healthcare centres (transferred from the NHS to PEDY), the urban primary (ex-EOPYY) health units that will remain in operation after restructuring, contracted doctors, private laboratories and other private primary healthcare units. As a recent study by the National School of Public Health has shown, the combined effect of all of the above measures is diminishing access to healthcare in Greece: six out of ten insured persons limited their use of EOPYY services because they could not afford co-payments (for visits and clinical tests, imposed in parallel with shrinking service coverage).[3]

In Italy, between 2009 and 2011, co-payments rose from 2.5 to 3.5 per cent of total public health spending (from €2.7 billion to about €4 billion [Giuliani & Cislaghi 2013]). The sharp increase was due to the introduction of new co-payments and the rise in previous ones. Recent studies (for example, Osservatorio sulla salute nelle regioni italiane 2013) argue that the NHS will not be able to hold in the near future if the co-payment rates increase. The Minister of Health himself, Balduzzi, declared in April 2013 to the media that the planned rises in co-payments will be practically untenable for many citizens (*La Repubblica* 2013).

*Controlling drug spending.* Policy measures have focused on lowering prices and quantities, with interventions: (a) on drug pricing and profit margins of providers, in parallel with administratively forced reduction of prices for specific drugs; and (b) on doctors prescribing patterns.

In the bailout countries, the revision of the price-setting systems resulted in significant cuts. In Portugal, in 2012, a new pricing methodology was established that defined as reference Spain, Slovenia and Italy (the latter two were replaced by France and Slovakia in 2013). In Greece, new regulations set as a basis the average rate of the three lowest-priced markets in the EU (22 countries are reference countries). Also, a number of drugs were eliminated from the so-called 'positive' list (that is, the list of drugs available on the NHS). In both countries profit margins of wholesalers and pharmacies were significantly curtailed, and new legislation made obligatory a clawback mechanism (if the budgeted ceiling for drugs expenditure is exceeded, the pharmaceutical industry will pay back the excess amount to the state). Due to large arrears in payments to providers by the national health systems, significant conflicts emerged leading to (long-lasting) strikes by pharmacists (e.g. in Greece), and failures in the supply chain.[4] This makes access to essential medicines difficult for patients, putting their lives at risk.

Increasing the market share of generics and regulating their prices are also major objectives stipulated by the MoUs. Prescription by drastic substance has been made mandatory in both countries.[5] In November 2013, a new law was passed by the Greek Parliament that cut the price of some generics and off-patent drugs, with the aim to further decrease drug spending by about €500 million (from €5.3 billion in 2009 to €2 billion in 2014 – so that pharmaceutical spending will be reduced to one per cent of GDP, as stipulated by the MoU).[6] This caused furious rows between the coalition government and the main opposition party, as the latter insisted that the cuts will have no effect on more expensive drugs to the benefit of multinational firms and to the detriment of patients.[7] The political clash reflects serious worries widely expressed by health experts that a drastic reduction of drug spending to one per cent of a GDP already slashed by a quarter (from 2009 to 2013) may lead to deficient coverage of the population with detrimental health effects.

In Italy the last few years have witnessed the attempt to match better control on drugs costs with more competition (and employment) in the sector. In particular, the Monti government tried to foster employment (allowing the opening of around 4,000 to 5,000 new pharmacies), price competition for drugs (among the new and old pharmacies and also with the drugstores – *parafarmacie* – for a series of drugs), more flexible opening hours and a lowering of the cost of drugs (general practitioners [GPs] will be obliged to advise their patients to use generics). Also, the 2011 'Finance Bill' introduced a partial financing by the pharmaceutical industries of the pharmaceutical deficits created by the NHS.

In Spain, the only legislation on cost control of drugs was enacted in March 2010 by reforming the reference price system, reducing the industrial price of generic drugs and promoting discounts in the profit margins of pharmacies. Also, in April 2012, the list of pharmaceuticals publicly financed was revised, so that some drugs were eliminated from the list.

*System reorganisation.* Compared with Greece, Portugal has succeeded in integrating a considerable part of primary care into the NHS and put in place a gatekeeping / referral system. Nevertheless, until recently about 15 per cent of the population was not registered with a family doctor.

In Greece, the amalgamation of the main health insurance funds in a single organisation (EOPYY) signposts a major change towards higher integration. A thorny issue, however, is how from some ailing health insurance funds, and with diminishing resources, adequate funding and quality of service provision by the unified primary healthcare system can be secured. Strikingly, a report by the Health Experts Committee submitted to the Minister of Health about three years ago warned that the planned 0.6 per cent of GDP as a subsidy to EOPYY was negligible, given that for IKA alone (the largest social insurance fund for employees) the subsidy (for health insurance) amounted to 1.2 per cent of GDP prior to the amalgamation. State subsidy further decreased to 0.4 per cent of GDP, which has shrunk considerably itself, as mentioned earlier. Another major predicament concerns diminishing contributions due to exceptionally high unemployment. All of this leads to the newly established national health insurance organisation being seriously underfunded.

Even if Italy and Spain have a more integrated primary and secondary care system, part of the recent attempts at reform aims to strengthen integration and, above all, to improve primary care and, consequently, to reduce waiting lists and pressure on emergency room departments and hospitals. In Italy, legislation enacted in 2012 (the so-called 'Balduzzi' Bill) focuses on improving the quality and the responsiveness of the NHS. Its major goal is to push forward a more de-hospitalised NHS with the creation of 'complex primary care units', fostering better integration among various healthcare professionals and an around-the-clock supply of outpatient services. This could be a significant step forward, but the problems so far have been on the financing side, as no additional economic resources have been granted to the NHS for the realisation of such an innovation.

In Spain, legislation passed in August 2011 included several measures to improve the quality and cohesion of the NHS, such as upgrading the health information system (individual health cards, clinic histories and electronic prescription), and the development of a coordination strategy for socio-sanitary care. The General Law on Public Health, enacted in October 2011, aims to improve preventive and promotional action in collective health, and labour and environmental health, and to clearly demarcate patients' rights and duties. However, the implementation of these pieces of legislation has been hindered by the need to reduce public expenditure.

*Downsizing.* The bailout agreements for Greece and Portugal embrace an array of measures for controlling cost (reining in hospital care expenditure and promoting economies of scale through service reorganisation). In Greece, reforms aim at the amalgamation of clinics and hospitals, or even the closing down of some healthcare units (4,000 'functional' beds have been eliminated according to the reorganisation plan).[8] Several mergers/closures of hospitals and departments have also already taken place in Portugal, leading to the elimination of about 1,000 beds, while in both countries the salaries of health personnel have been significantly reduced. As for hospital services costing and payment, Portugal adopted the DRGs (Diagnosis Related Groups) costing system as early as 1990 and has developed it further over recent decades. In Greece a shift from retrospective reimbursement based on the patient cost per speciality to case-mix-based payment took place in 2011, but is still at an incipient stage (Skroubelos et al. 2012).

In both countries, administrative staff shortages are intensifying due, among other reasons, to the policy of layoffs and recruitment freezing with the aim of considerably shrinking the public sector in the coming years. In Greece, about a quarter of intensive care beds are not in operation due to shortages of health personnel (particularly of nursing staff).[9] Moreover, unemployment among doctors has sharply increased during the crisis, and a wave of emigration by medical doctors and nurses to Western Europe (mostly Germany, but also Brazil for Portuguese health professionals) has intensified.[10]

Similarly, in Italy, downsizing the hospital sector and restructuring secondary care are at the forefront of recent reforms. A new target requires the reduction of the number of beds per 1,000 inhabitants from 4.0 to 3.7 and the hospitalisation rate from 18 to 16 per cent.

The pay and hiring freeze of healthcare personnel, legislated with the 2011 'Finance Bill', could create even bigger problems for the future of the Italian NHS. In particular the association representing public hospital doctors (Associazione Nazionale Aiuti Assistenti Ospedalieri - Associazione Medici Dirigenti [ANAAO-ASSOMED]) produced a study expressing worries about the (near) future. The ANAAO-ASSOMED (2011) estimated that by 2021 around 30,000 doctors will have retired (nowadays there are around 105,000 doctors in the NHS) and, even more importantly, in specific fields there is going to be a decrease in doctors of 25 per cent (paediatricians, surgeons and internal medicine specialists). Elaborating data from the Ministry of Finance, the ANAAO-ASSOMED denounces also the increase in the precariousness of labour contracts: from 2001 to 2011 the number of doctors working for the NHS with fixed-term contracts doubled (from 3,700 to 7,300). The choice of flexibilisation of contracts and salary freezing indicates an important change in the sector.

In Greece, Portugal and Italy, measures were also introduced in order to increase competition among private providers. In particular two parallel measures have been followed over the last couple of years: price reductions on some services provided by private entities, e.g. imaging, laboratory tests, etc., and new, centralised procurement mechanisms to induce competition among private providers. In Italy, the plan has been also to cut contracts with private providers in order to reduce supply and to better control costs, while in Greece a clawback mechanism for private clinics and diagnostic health units (similar to that in force for pharmaceutical providers) was put in place in 2013.

In contrast, little has happened in the Spanish case, with the exception of the already stated cut in salaries of healthcare professionals, the freezing of new contracts and an expansion of working hours. However, although information is scant, since 2011 regional healthcare systems have begun to introduce an array of restrictive measures such as reducing hospital beds, utilisation of operating theatres, and diagnostic tests. Some regions have even sold health centres and/or eliminated attention services for patients in emergency units. Privatisation of the management of some hospitals has also taken place in several regions.

*Where is Health Reform Heading?*

Table 5 summarises the main changes introduced according to whether they shift the cost to the patient, seek efficiency savings through multiple changes in system organisation and governance and/or promote cuts in labour costs.

**Table 5** Summary of Policy Change

| | Shifting the cost to the patient (effects on access and equity) (A) | | | Seeking cost savings through changes in system governance (effects mostly on efficiency and sustainability) (B) | | | | | | Cutting labour costs (effects on quality) (C) | |
|---|---|---|---|---|---|---|---|---|---|---|---|
| | User charges | Cuts in service provisions | Control of drugs expenditure (mandatory International Nonproprietory Name [INN] prescription and other measures) | Price regulation of pharmaceutical markets / clawback / caps in spending | Tighter control of procurement | Primary & secondary care integration | E-diagnosis / clinical protocols / E-prescribing / DRGs | Reorganisation / downsizing of hospitals | Price regulation of contracted-out provision | Downsizing personnel | Freezing of salaries / Cuts in salaries |
| Greece | ++ | ++ | ++* | ++ | + | + | ++ | ++ | ++ | ++ | ++ |
| Portugal | ++ | + | + | ++ | + | + | ++ | +(+) | ++ | + | +(+) |
| Italy | +(+) | +** | +(+) | ++ | + | =/+ | + | + | ++ | + | +(+) |
| Spain | + | + | + | + | = | = | = | + (in some regions) | = | = | +(+) |

*Notes:* = no changes; + some changes; +(+) significant changes; ++ very significant changes.

*As mentioned above, if patients choose the brand name drug, they must pay the difference between the cost of the latter and the lowest-priced generic (on top of the 25 per cent co-payment). It is noteworthy that Greece continues to score high regarding under-the-table payments. In contrast, in Portugal and Spain informal payments are virtually non-existent, and in Italy they are not a very frequent phenomenon (Health Consumer Powerhouse [HCP] 2013, pp. 72–73).

**Mostly due to long waiting lists and cuts in hospital beds.

As indicated in column B, to one extent or another all four countries have introduced measures for rationalising spending and strengthening the longer-term sustainability of the system. Changes in system governance have been introduced, to a varying degree, and steps have been taken to downsize the hospital sector and boost efficiency (measured with respect to physical/financial inputs and specific outcomes, such as discharges, inpatient days, inpatient procedures performed, etc.). A heavy strain on workforce capacity is also evident.

In the bailout countries (and also in Italy), efficiency savings have been accompanied with measures shifting a progressively larger part of the cost to the patient through increasing fees and co-payments and reviewing downwards the range of public provision. Greece exhibits by far the highest decline in public health spending per capita (by over 30 per cent between 2009 and 2012, in real terms, as defined in Table 3 above).

If we also take into account that the crisis is excluding from the SE national health systems a rising number of individuals – sometimes as an implicit consequence of rationing, other times as an explicit result of policy choices – we come up with a bleak outlook in terms of access, equity and fairness. For instance, as an explicit choice, in the case of Greece there is an alarmingly increasing number of uninsured people, estimated to be close to two-and-a-half million people (according to the latest data provided by EOPYY), due to dramatically rising unemployment and a large number of the self-employed unable to continue paying contributions. As a result of implicit consequences of rationing, there is evidence from Italy, Greece and Portugal that points towards a reduction in the use of services due to higher co-payment costs and system bottlenecks (long waiting lists and often a lack of medical supplies, particularly in Greece).

Importantly, none of the four countries has so far overtly promoted the marketisation (and privatisation) of healthcare. Instead, the politico-ideological framing of the reform uses a controversial language stressing the need for deep cuts as a tool to keep the publicly operated systems alive.

The two largest countries have so far been dealing with the crisis through fiscal and organisational fine-tuning (a 'recalibration' strategy). However, in Italy, potentially deeper cuts in the future, in tandem with increasing employment insecurity, may soon deal a serious blow to public healthcare. In the two smaller countries, controversial measures are applied equalising coverage but at the same time levelling quality and provision downwards to a low common denominator. This indeed reflects a drift towards limited state responsibility in healthcare (a public system covering only basic medical necessities), albeit at a time when a large number of households are in dire financial straits and can hardly access any complementary insurance in the market. This puts at risk not only the most vulnerable groups but also the health of large sections of the population.

### The Impact of Austerity-Driven Reforms on Health: An Initial Assessment

In the last decade life expectancy at the age of 65 has increased in all four countries while the mean number of healthy life years has significantly diminished (Table 6).

**Table 6** Life Expectancy and Healthy Life Years at the Age of 65

| | Women | | | | Men | | | |
|---|---|---|---|---|---|---|---|---|
| | 2004 | | 2012 | | 2004 | | 2012 | |
| | Life expectancy | Healthy life years | Life expectancy | Healthy life years* | Life expectancy | Healthy life years | Life expectancy | Healthy life years* |
| Greece | 19.8 | 9.5 | 21.0 | 7.3 | 16.9 | 9.5 | 18.1 | 8.6 |
| Italy | 21.3 | 12.5 | 22.1 | 7.2 | 17.3 | 11.4 | 18.5 | 7.8 |
| Portugal | 20.0 | 3.8 | 21.3 | 6.3 | 16.3 | 5.1 | 17.6 | 7.8 |
| Spain | 21.4 | 9.6 | 22.8 | 9.0 | 17.2 | 9.8 | 18.7 | 9.2 |
| EU-27** | 20.0 | 8.9 | 21.2 | 8.9 | 16.3 | 8.6 | 17.6 | 8.7 |

*Source*: Eurostat data, available online at: http://epp.eurostat.ec.europa.eu/portal/page/portal/statistics/themes.
*Notes*: *For Portugal data refer to 2011; **For EU-27 healthy life years refer to 2005 and 2010.

This trend characterises especially Italy and Greece. Estimations by the Greek National School of Public Health indicate a heavy toll of austerity on the health of the population, as life expectancy at birth is forecast to decrease by three years during the current decade (see note 3). Healthy life years at the age of 65 increased only in Portugal but figures still remain below the EU-27 average. The decline is negligible in Spain, which persistently records a higher number of healthy life years than the EU-27 average (and than the other three SE countries).

Infant mortality rates are comparatively low (3.2–3.5 per 1,000 live births in SE countries vs. 3.9 in the EU-27) and have improved over the 2000s, but a slight reversal of the trend has been recorded in the last few years in Greece (in tandem with a small increase in underweight newborns, recorded in Portugal as well).[11] Moreover, as recently indicated by the president of the Médecins du Monde, Greece is close to 'tearing down the vaccination barrier in the country', as thousands of children are left unvaccinated.[12]

Cancer treatment is underfunded in Greece and Portugal. There are long waiting lists and diminishing support. Moreover, decisions about licensing and pricing new drugs particularly for serious illnesses are greatly delayed in both countries. A report by IOBE (the Foundation for Economic and Industrial Research [Kyriopoulos, Maniadakis & Stournaras 2011]) indicates a significant reduction of expenditure for drugs that help treat serious illnesses in Greece (for Portugal see Araújo et al. 2009). In Greece, cardiovascular diseases, mental disorders and some infectious diseases (like malaria) are on the increase, as are 'unhealthy practices' (like alcohol and drug abuse) (Kondilis et al. 2013). There is also evidence of an increasing suicide rate (up by about 40 per cent between 2009 and mid-2012), partly the consequence of dramatic cuts in mental healthcare (Economou et al. 2012). Furthermore, cutbacks in drug addiction treatment have caused a ten-fold increase in HIV cases by injecting drug-users between 2004 and late 2011 (Paraskevis et al. 2011).

**Table 7** Unmet Need for a Medical Examination ('Too Expensive', 'Waiting List' or 'Too far to Travel'), 2006/12

| | 2006 | | | | 2012 | | | |
|---|---|---|---|---|---|---|---|---|
| | Bottom quintile | | Middle quintile | | Bottom quintile | | Middle quintile | |
| | Total | 75 + yrs | Total | 75 + yrs | Total | 75 + yrs | Total | 75 + yrs |
| Greece | 7.5 | 9.0 | 7.1 | 14.4 | 11.6 | 12.4 | 9.2 | 18.2 |
| Italy | 9.1 | 8.3 | 4.0 | 6.0 | 11.6 | 13.8 | 5.4 | 6.6 |
| Spain | 0.9 | 1.9 | 0.5 | 0.2 | 1.3 | 2.3 | 0.8 | 0.2 |
| Portugal | 9.1 | 13.2 | 4.9 | 6.1 | 5.7 | 7.2 | 3.0 | 4.4 |
| EU-27 | 7.2 | 6.2 | 3.7 | 4.6 | 5.9 | 6.6 | 3.0 | 4.8 |

*Source:* As in Table 6.

Diminishing access to healthcare is evident mostly in Greece and to a lesser extent in Italy. In Greece, the percentage of people in the bottom and middle income quintiles who reported that they were unable to meet needs for medical examination (because it was 'too expensive', 'too far' or there were 'waiting lists') has risen over the last few years. However, in both countries barriers to access are higher among elderly people (75-year-olds and over [Table 7]). Strikingly, in Greece, in 2012, over nine per cent of the population in the middle income quintile reported unmet needs for medical examination (and about one in five 75-year-olds and over in this income quintile). In Italy 12 per cent of individuals in the bottom quintile reported unmet medical needs in 2012 (almost 14 per cent among the 75 and over population). In Spain the extent of unmet need has been negligible. Portugal records a substantial improvement as self-reported need for medical examination decreased in the second half of the 2000s.

The manifold ways in which the crisis and austerity affect health conditions is outside the scope of our analysis. Besides, as stressed earlier, a longer time span is required for many of the effects (and their scope and depth) to become clearly visible. Here we have briefly reviewed some available health indicators in an attempt to highlight the potential consequences of cutbacks in health spending so far. In tune with what we argued earlier, health indicators render support to our argument that, in Spain, the policies adopted under the crisis conditions consist mostly in piecemeal adjustment/recalibration in a way that universal access to a broad range of publicly provided services has so far been maintained, although data for the years in which budgetary cuts were strongest (2012–14) and subsequent years are not yet available and, thus, the impact of these is yet to be seen. Also, in Italy, the reforms undertaken and the cuts introduced over the last few years have been comparatively modest. Nevertheless, some health indicators have worsened (unmet need has significantly increased and healthy life years for the population aged 65 and over have diminished). Severe cuts and structural changes drastically reducing public provision have seriously affected health conditions in Greece, while in Portugal the findings seem to be controversial: unmet need has declined and healthy life years for the elderly increased, but some birth-related indicators have worsened. Notably, increasing barriers of access to prevention and healthcare (especially in Greece) may cause an eruption of expensive morbidity in the future which is highly likely to have a boomerang effect on fiscal retrenchment.

## Conclusion

The above analysis has tried to highlight the healthcare reform trajectories in SE during the crisis. Although all four SE countries developed NHSs in the past, significant differences persisted on account of crucial criteria of universal access, equity and funding (Guillén 2002). Italy and Spain achieved a higher degree of system integration and a decentralised mode of managing funding and delivery, and kept private expenditure low. Yet, on the basis of citizens' assessment of the extent and quality of universal coverage, with the exception of Spain, dissatisfaction was high even before the crisis. The Italian NHS showed some problems in this respect, while Portugal and Greece registered serious deficiencies and comparatively higher inequalities. This distinction is cross-cut by trends in health spending: between 2000 and 2008, Greece and Spain exhibited a rapid expansion of public spending (in Greece, mostly due to galloping medication expenditure), while in Italy and Portugal the trend was moderate. However, Italy remains the highest per capita spender of the four countries. The crisis and austerity have greatly increased dissatisfaction with healthcare provision in Greece. Negative assessment by citizens has also risen moderately in Italy and remained widely prevalent in Portugal, in contrast with Spain, where citizens' appraisal remained overwhelmingly positive until late 2013. Nonetheless, data on satisfaction and on subjective appraisals of unmet need must always be regarded with caution, given that the responses of citizens are very sensitive to differences in expectations and political cultures.

Fiscal sustainability has been the main leverage of reform under the crisis. Even though none of the four countries has openly embarked upon systemic change dismantling the public system, the austerity-driven measures applied so far (and further changes planned for the coming years) may add up to a transformative process in both the funding and provision sides of the SE health systems. In the bailout countries controversy permeates reforms. Some measures are in the right direction in tackling serious functional and financial problems. Yet the imperative of fiscal restraint triggers a kind of 'policy drift' and/or exhaustion, whereby the publicly operating system gradually withers away. Apparently, large-scale public spending cutbacks and a range of policy measures are shifting the cost of care away from the state.

In Italy, the gap between the original aims of a universal NHS and its actual effects on barriers to access and worsening quality was evident before the crisis begun. Fiscal retrenchment is further fuelling the erosion of the public system. In Spain public expenditure cuts were relevant but the data on outcomes seem to suggest that austerity-driven reforms have so far (and only so far) had a moderate impact. Moreover, in this latter case, increasing differences among regional healthcare systems and a mounting tension between professionals and governments are among the negative aspects of the management of the crisis.

In Greece and Portugal the scale of retrenchment and the accompanying reforms indicate a major rethink (even if not explicitly formulated) of the financial and institutional assumptions of publicly operated health systems. Whether this is an irreversible trend is an open question, though there have been no signs so far of balancing fiscal savings and efficiency gains with attempts to improve access and quality. Instances of healthcare restructuring in Europe even before the crisis – for example the marketisation of health insurance in the Netherlands in 2006, or even in Sweden (the bastion of the social-democratic welfare state) the shift of a large part of primary healthcare to private providers in 2006 (Saltman & Cahn 2013) – make a scenario of drastic retrenchment of public healthcare provision in SE countries highly likely. Alarmingly, such a development may exacerbate health inequality, due to the unequal ability of people to seek complementary insurance in the market and also because of scant guarantees for effective state regulation of private sector stakeholders.

## Acknowledgements

We would like to thank Berta Álvarez-Miranda and Amílcar Moreira for their useful comments on draft versions of this article.

## Notes

1. Own elaboration from Istat 2007 and 2012 microdata on household consumption expenditure.
2. For example, in Greece new regulations of EOPYY (the unified health insurance organisation that emerged out of the amalgamation of a number of health insurance funds in 2011, and with the 2014 reform turned into a purchaser of health services), among others, limited the number of physiotherapy and logotherapy sessions per year, drastically reduced cost reimbursement for kidney failure patients' transport to undergo hemocatharsis treatment, and introduced caps on microbiological and screening tests (see EOPYY website at: http://www.eopyy.gov.gr/).
3. Data obtained from the National School of Public Health.
4. According to the 'Grieving Pharmacies' movement in Portugal, 1,300 pharmacies have had their supplies suspended and about 600 pharmacies were facing closure in 2013 (latest study by the Nova School; see: http://www.theportugalnews.com/news/students-join-fight-for-portugals-pharmacies/26964). Equally, in Greece, four in ten pharmacies are facing closure (information obtained from the Panhellenic Pharmaceutical Association). In the last few years drug shortages have been a recurrent phenomenon in both countries.
5. In Greece, on top of the existing user charges, patients are charged 100 per cent of the extra cost if they choose to buy the brand name instead of the least expensive generic. Drastic cuts in drug spending have also been accompanied by great delays and/or restrictiveness in the introduction of novel, patented (expensive) drugs for serious illnesses (see HCP 2013, p. 16)
6. A similar target has also been set for Portugal.
7. It will also hurt Greek pharmaceutical firms producing generics, as competition from low wage countries (some of them producing medicines of dubious quality) may drive them out of the market.
8. Out of the 137 public hospitals, 83 entities now exist as a result of mergers. Also, from a total of 1,950 clinics in public hospitals 330 were merged (and 40 were transferred between hospitals). Moreover, 550 beds were allocated to private practice. The changes are forecast to save about

€150 million in the context of the medium-term plan (data obtained from the Ministry of Health). Reorganisation and closure of some primary healthcare units previously under EOPYY are also underway.

9. Greece, Spain and Portugal exhibit the lowest density of nursing staff in Europe (3.3, 4.9 and 5.7 per 1,000 inhabitants, respectively; compared, for instance, with 11 in Germany and 14.8 in Denmark; in Italy the ratio was 6.3). In all four countries, however, the respective ratios for doctors have been among the highest in Europe (6.1 in Greece, 3.8 in Portugal and Spain and 3.7 in Italy; EU-27 average: 3.4 [OECD 2013]).

10. According to the Athens Medical Association (see: http://www.isathens.gr/syllogos/arxeio-drasewn-isa/arxeio-syndikalistiko/2240-iatriki-metanastefsi-isa-anergia.html), about a third of doctors in Athens are unemployed or underemployed), while the number of specialists who emigrated in 2012 increased fivefold in comparison with 2007. For Portugal see: http://blogs. bmj.com/bmj/2013/06/27/tiago-villanueva-why-does-brazil-want-to-recruit-doctors-from-spain-and-portugal/

11. Eurostat and OECD data retrieved from http://epp.eurostat.ec.europa.eu/portal/page/portal/ eurostat/home/ and http://www.oecd-ilibrary.org/statistics, respectively.

12. See: http://greece.greekreporter.com/2013/12/05/thousands-of-children-in-greece-unvaccinated/. Austerity has significantly reduced resources for free vaccination programmes for children whose parents cannot afford to pay.

## References

ANAAO-ASSOMED (2011) *Il futuro economico dei Dirigenti medici e sanitari e del Ssn*, ANAAO, Rome.

Araújo, A., Barata, F., Barroso, S., Cortes, P., Damasceno, M., Parreira, A., Espírito Santo, J., Teixeira, E. & Pereira, P. (2009) 'Custo do tratamento do cancro em Portugal', *Acta Médica Portuguesa*, vol. 22, no. 5, pp. 525–536.

Barros, P. P. (2012) 'Health policy reform in tough times: the case of Portugal', *Health Policy*, vol. 106, no. 1, pp. 17–22.

Barros, P. P., Machado, S. R. & de Almeida Simões, J. (2011) 'Portugal: health system review'. European Observatory on Health Systems and Policies, available online at: http://www.euro. who.int/__data/assets/pdf_file/0019/150463/e95712.pdf

Davaki, D. & Mossialos, E. (2006) 'Financing and delivering health care', in *Social Policy Developments in Greece*, eds M. Petmesidou & E. Mossialos, Ashgate, Aldershot, pp. 286–318.

Economou, M., Madianos, M., Peppou, L. E., Theleritis, C. N. & Stefanis, C. (2012) 'Suicidality and the economic crisis in Greece', *The Lancet*, vol. 380, no. 9839, p. 337.

Fundación FOESSA-Cáritas (2014) *Desigualdad y derechos sociales. Análisis y perspectivas 2013*, Fundación FOESSA, Madrid.

El Economista, 21st October 2013.

Giuliani, F. & Cislaghi, C. (2013) *La misura attuale a livello nazionale del Copayment in Sanità*, Agenas, Roma.

Guillén, A. M. (2002) 'The politics of universalisation: establishing National Health Services in Southern Europe', *West European Politics*, vol. 25, no. 4, pp. 49–68.

Hacker, J. S. (2004) 'Privatizing risk without privatizing the welfare state: the hidden politics of social policy retrenchment in the United States', *American Political Science Review*, vol. 98, no. 2, pp. 243–260.

HCP (Health Consumer Powerhouse) (2013) 'Euro Health Consumer Index 2013', available online at: http://www.healthpowerhouse.com/index.php?Itemid=55

INE (Instituto Nacional de Estadística) (2011) *Encuesta de Presupuestos Familiares 2007–2010*, INE, Madrid.

Kondilis, E., Giannakopoulos, S., Gavana, M., Ierodiakonou, I., Waitzkin, H. & Benos, A. (2013) 'Economic crisis, restrictive policies, and the population's health and health care: the Greek case', *American Journal of Public Health*, vol. 103, no. 6, pp. 973–979.

Kyriopoulos, J., Maniadakis, N. & Stournaras, J. (2011) *Δαπάνες Υγείας και Πολιτικές Υγείας την Περίοδο του Μνημονίου*, [Health Expenditure and Health Policies at the 'Memorandum' Era], IOBE, Athens.

La Repubblica. (2013) 'Quattro milioni in fuga dalle cure'. Rome, available online at: http://inchieste. repubblica.it/it/repubblica/rep-it/inchiesta-italiana/2013/04/25/news/quattro_milioni_in_ fuga_dalle_cure_non_hanno_pi_i_soldi_per_il_ticket-57450028/

OECD (2012) *Health at a Glance*, OECD, Paris.

OECD (2013) *Health at a Glance*, OECD, Paris.

Osservatorio sulla salute nelle regioni italiane. (2013) 'Rapporto Osservasalute 2012'. Rome, available online at: http://www.osservasalute.it/

Paraskevis, D., Nikolopoulos, G., Tsiara, C., Paraskeva, D., Antoniadou, A., Lazanas, M., Gargalianos, P., Psychogiou, M., Malliori, M., Kremastinou, J. & Hatzakis, A. (2011) 'HIV-1 outbreak among injecting drug users in Greece', *Euro Surveillance*, vol. 16, no. 36, pp. 1–4.

Pavolini, E. & Guillén, A. (eds) (2013) *Health Care Systems in Europe under Austerity. Institutional Reforms and Performance*, Palgrave, Basingstoke.

Petmesidou, M. (2013a) 'Southern Europe', in *International Handbook of the Welfare State*, ed. B. Greve, Routledge, London, pp. 183–192.

Petmesidou, M. (2013b) 'Is social protection in Greece at a crossroads?', *European Societies*, vol. 15, no. 4, pp. 597–616.

Petmesidou, M. & Guillén, A. M. (2008) "Southern-style' national health services? Recent reforms and trends in Spain and Greece', *Social Policy and Administration*, vol. 42, no. 2, pp. 106–124.

Petmesidou, M., Papatheodorou, C., Papanastasiou, S., Moisidou, A. & Pempetzoglou, M. (2014) *Healhcare Reform in Greece. Interim Report*, Observatory on Economic and Social Developments, INE-GSEE, Athens.

Pierson, P. (1994) *Dismantling the Welfare State? Reagan, Thatcher, and the Politics of Retrenchment*, Cambridge University Press, New York.

Saltman, R. & Cahn, Z. (2013) 'Restructuring health systems for an era of prolonged austerity', *BMJ*, vol. 347, pp. 17–19.

Skroubelos, A., Kapaki, V., Athanassakis, C., Souliotis, K. & Kyriopoulos, J. (2012) *Ανασυγκρότηση και Χρηματοδότηση της Ασφάλισης Υγείας*, [Restructuring and Funding of Health Insurance], National School for Public Health, Athens.

Streeck, W. & Thelen, K. (2005) *Beyond Continuity: Institutional Change in Advanced Political Economies*, Oxford University Press, Oxford.

# 'Social Investment' or Back to 'Familism': The Impact of the Economic Crisis on Family and Care Policies in Italy and Spain

Margarita León and Emmanuele Pavolini

*Family policies have traditionally been weak in Southern Europe. In the last two decades, however, and following a 'catching up' course, Spain has created new family programmes and expanded existing ones. Meanwhile, the picture for Italy during the years preceding the crisis is more of a 'frozen landscape'. However, the diverging paths of the two countries in terms of policy reform in the years preceding the crisis do not place them in substantially different positions. The economic crisis and the austerity measures that followed have aggravated the weaknesses of family and care policies in both countries.*

Welfare state dynamics of transformation are, as argued by Bonoli and Natali (2012), multifaceted and multidimensional. In an attempt to characterise change in family and care policies before and after the financial crisis, we refer to the concept of retrenchment and recalibration. 'Retrenchment' usually indicates a situation of substantial cuts to specific policies. Pierson (1998) defines retrenchment as a situation where, firstly, there is a significant increase in the reliance on means-testing; secondly, there are major transfers of responsibility to the private sector; and, thirdly, there are dramatic changes in benefit and eligibility rules that signal a qualitative reform of a particular programme. Along with the possibility of retrenchment, the concept of 'recalibration' has been introduced in the literature since the turn of the century. Ferrera, Hemerijck & Rhodes (2000) define recalibration as an extensive form of welfare state remodelling along four key dimensions: functional, distributive, normative and institutional recalibration. Recalibration can be seen as a potential adaptive response to changes in the socio-economic context taking place in recent decades and it is linked to the question of how to improve policy performance under conditions of structural environmental change.

The issue of recalibration is closely connected to the more recent debate on social investment (Morel, Palier & Palme 2012). In this approach, human capital building, the fight against the intergenerational reproduction of inequalities, and gender equality are essential social policy objectives. Under this perspective, family policies become powerful tools to enhance the achievement of such goals.

The present paper aims to frame the evolution of family and care policies in Italy and Spain over the last two decades, taking into consideration the retrenchment/recalibration debate, as well as empirical studies on the stage of development of a social investment approach. Have these countries followed a common trajectory or can alternative routes be identified? What has been the impact of the economic crisis in these policy fields?

## Understanding Policy Change in the Italian and Spanish Welfare States

Spain and Italy have traditionally shared a similar overall structure of their welfare systems. That is, an institutional design organised around, first, a Bismarckian model in pensions, unemployment and labour market policies; second, a Universalistic model in education and health; and, third, a rather limited intervention model in social assistance, social care and family support. Therefore, from the outset, a defining feature of these countries' welfare models has been a mixture of different institutional principles. This combination of principles together with other unique features made Ferrera (1996) propose in his seminal article that countries of Southern Europe deserved a welfare regime type of their own. With many different variants, several scholars have identified these 'via media' (Moreno 2001) traits as a strong driver towards the clustering of these countries of the south together. Other authors have instead argued that welfare states in countries of Southern Europe are no more than a variant of the conservative-corporatist regime type (Esping-Andersen 1999) and that some of the attributed features may have been underspecified (Guillén & León 2011; Guillén 2010).

In any case, there does not seem to be any fundamental controversy when it comes to the familistic character of social policies in the four Mediterranean countries and the pervasiveness of the male-breadwinner model, acting as strong barriers for the expansion of social care and family policies. In this respect, several scholars have emphasised the importance of cultural traditions and social norms embedded in Catholicism with regards to family values and gender roles in the shaping of welfare states of the South (Pfau-Effinger 1998). While conservative-corporatist welfare states such as Germany and Austria have also deserved the familistic label, the key difference between the countries of Central and Southern Europe is that in the former the male-breadwinner model has been maintained through family and fiscal policies that facilitated, if not encouraged, the role of women as carers in the private domain, whereas in the latter familism has largely been 'unsupported' (Keck & Saraceno 2010), meaning a strange kind of subsidiarity principle whereby such familistic culture is in fact the justification for the residual character of this policy domain (León 2002; Flaquer 2000; Valiente 1996).

However, the presence of familism as a defining category of Southern European welfare states more generally is often taken for granted in comparative analysis of welfare systems, neglecting both intra-country variation and change over time (León & Migliavacca 2013; Guillén & León 2011). And yet, and as the following section will show, Spain and Italy have seldom gone through recalibration/retrenchment phases over recent years with regard to this traditionally marginal policy field. Although the performance of the two countries was to a certain extent different in the decade preceding the economic crisis, the austerity measures introduced, especially since 2010, have hit both countries equally hard.


## Family and Care Policies before the Outbreak of the Crisis in Spain and Italy: A Fertile Land and a Quasi-Frozen Landscape

Since the 1990s limited new social rights relating to family and care issues have been established in Italy. Moreover, no relevant national plans to strengthen higher coverage rates have been put forward. Although some important legislative initiatives were produced, these usually fell short. Quite often, reforms lacked adequate financial resources in order to be implemented and to have a potential useful impact in the coverage of needs (Da Roit & Sabatinelli 2013; Kazepov 2010; Maino & Neri 2011). In particular, in the late 1990s to early 2000s four relevant acts were passed, but all of them showed shortcomings.

In 1997 a law on children's welfare (law 285) promoted, among other interventions, care services, but only limited financial resources were provided for its implementation. The result has been the development of a variety of initiatives although neither their stability over time was ensured nor their capacity to deeply tackle care needs (Da Roit & Sabatinelli 2013). In 1999 a special family allowance for low income families with at least three underage children was established. However, the low level of benefits and the high threshold adopted were only able to address poverty intensity rather than reducing poverty (Da Roit & Sabatinelli 2013). In 2000 a law on parental leave was passed, introducing relevant innovation (the possibility to fraction flexibly the leave period, and the incentive for uptake by fathers). However, in this case there were also limitations in terms of relevance and coverage of care needs which this new piece of legislation offered (in particular in relation to duration and replacement rates) (Naldini & Saraceno 2008).

The most promising reform passed in those years was Law 328 in 2000. This legislation was relatively good in terms of principles and general aims. In particular, it stated the idea of national 'basic levels of social intervention' (LEAs) to be guaranteed everywhere in different policy areas and for several types of intervention. However, these LEAs had two major shortcomings: they were vaguely defined, ending up not having any practical impact, and not enough resources were dedicated to implement them (in particular, no new mechanism was created in order to guarantee adequate funding for providing less residual social care and services). Moreover, the

Constitutional reform in 2001 transferred more power to Regions and local authorities (but not more autonomous funding tools), leaving the state with more limited tasks.

The 2000s witnessed even less legislative production and also the development of a limited political debate about how to reform family policies. A centre-right government ruled for most of the decade (a centre-left government was in charge only for around one year and a half between 2006 and 2008). During its first five years of government (2001–06) the Berlusconi government intervened in family policies only in two ways in 2002–03. On the one hand, it lowered the threshold for entering kindergarten with bill no. 53. This legislation introduced the possibility for children aged two years and a half to enter kindergarten (instead of three years of age, as the previous legislation prescribed). The idea was to offer more statutory coverage in the 0–3 age range, without investing in early childcare facilities but lowering the entry age into pre-school. On the other hand, the National Budget Planning Law for 2003 introduced the possibility of financing firms' crèches and similar childcare services.

The centre-left government during its short term in government sought, instead, to develop more traditional childcare facilities, investing around €800 million (with a partial co-financing by regional authorities) for a National Extraordinary Crèches Plan with the aim of improving coverage by four per cent of children under the age of three (Sabatinelli 2010).

The last centre-right government in the first years of the crisis before austerity plans were introduced (2008–09) announced some innovations (the financing of tele-work, more support for parental leave and small family-style care services) but it did not carry them out.

If in the last two decades there was limited innovation (and new financing) in the field of family policies in the realm of childcare, even less took place in elderly care. In the mid-1990s a national commission for the reform of the whole Italian welfare system (the Commissione Onofri) proposed an in-depth review of the disability support scheme and to introduce a new long-term care (LTC) scheme. The idea was to go beyond an LTC system based mainly on cash benefits (the 'Companion's Allowance') and to develop a more integrated approach mixing services and economic transfers. The proposal was never taken seriously into consideration in the following years and remained largely ignored.

The only real long-term care policy that Italian governments were able to foster was indirect support of the care labour market through a mix between recognition of the role of migrant work in this field (in terms of regularisation of illegal foreign care workers, in 2002 and 2009, and of the setting of yearly quotas for migrant flows for care work) and the substantial acceptance of irregular work done by migrants in many households (the controls on the regularity of working contracts when families hire migrant carers have been quite limited over time) (Costa 2012). The result was that until the crisis Italy still presented a relatively low level of needs coverage in the main social care fields, namely childcare and elderly care (Ascoli & Pavolini 2012).

If nothing took place at a national level, other stakeholders and levels of government were slightly more dynamic with regard to family policies and their attempt to 'modernise from below'. In particular, a set of interested parties has been trying to innovate: local governments; companies and trade unions; families and the third sector.

Firstly, thanks to the decentralisation process that was developed in recent decades in Italy, local authorities and Regions have developed more and more new ways to tackle family policy issues (Andreotti, Mingione & Polizzi 2012). The result has been an increase in local childcare and elderly care coverage also thanks to partnerships with the third sector and other private providers. Frequently, this increase in coverage rate has taken place due to funds coming directly from local authorities and not the national state: in 2010 around 63 per cent of the local authorities' social expenditure came directly from their own sources (direct taxation) and this incidence has increased over the last decade (Istat 2013). Secondly, enterprises and trade unions were other important stakeholders in this attempt to modernise Italian family policies from below. Occupational welfare, as defined by Titmuss, is becoming increasingly relevant in the Italian welfare system and is playing a new role in family policies (Pavolini, Ascoli & Mirabile 2013). In comparison with the 1990s there has been a strong increase in recent years in industry- and company-level family policies, often discussed between firms, trade unions and local authorities: the request of flexibility required by companies is matched more and more by the needs of many employees to better conciliate work with personal and family issues. Company-owned or company-funded kindergartens or crèches, other forms of professional help for childcare or for care for workers' elderly parents, extra-statutory parental leave, and extra-statutory sickness leave when children or other close relatives are sick or have disabilities are all becoming more often associated with collective bargaining at company level or industrial sector level.

Thirdly, the final party that has tried to cope with the 'national frozen landscape' are the families directly in need of help for care. In the absence of any real support from the State, households have discovered the market. In childcare a significant part of the increase in coverage since the 1990s can be attributed to private providers not connected to local public provision. European Union Statistics on Income and Living Conditions (EU-SILC) data for 2010 estimate for Italy a coverage rate of around 25 per cent of children under three years old going to formal childcare (see Table 2). Istat for the same year calculates 14 per cent of public coverage. The difference between these two values provides an estimate of the relevance of private provision (around ten per cent) of total coverage. If the private market covers a significant part of the demand in childcare, the situation is even more pronounced in elderly and long-term care. In the latter case migrant care work has become a central feature since the second part of the 1990s. Recent studies estimate the presence of at least 700,000 foreign care workers in Italy. This figure equals 81.5 per cent of the overall labour force in the field (Costa 2012).

The narrative is partially different in the case of Spain in that since the early 1990s there has been a strong 'catching up' impulse that led centre-right (Aznar 1996–2004) and centre-left (Zapatero 2004–11) governments to introduce policies addressing new social risks and to remove elements of social protection linked to the prescriptions of the male-breadwinner model. The scope for the introduction of new family and care policies was large determined by, on the one hand, the general inaction of previous governments in this policy field since the beginning of democracy and, on the other hand, the cross-political party consensus on the need to promote egalitarian legislation and institutional adaptation to move away from the image of women as 'angels of the home' (Valiente 2013; León 2011). However, the assessment of actual outcomes of new pieces of legislation and programmes in care and family policies shows limited impact in terms of scope and capacity for redistribution. As will be shown, some of the recently created instruments have a rather symbolic value and, in any case, the budgetary cuts that have been introduced since 2010 have strongly affected these policies of more recent creation.

Let us look first at childcare, where great improvement in terms of coverage and also in terms of the quality of the provision came with the National Organic Law of Education of 1990, which introduced pre-school as three non-compulsory years but fully universal and subject to the same regulations and conditions as elementary schooling. This was clearly a catching up process with countries such as France and Italy. The latter established state responsibility for the three years of pre-school back in 1968 (law 1444) (Ranci & Sabatinelli, 2014). Interestingly enough, Italy and Spain name these pre-school years in the same way (*scuole dell'infanzia* in Italy and *educación infantil* in Spain, which literally translated means 'infant schools'). In Spain, as had already been the case in Italy, the universalisation of pre-school enabled its consolidation in terms of enrolment (virtually 100 per cent of children start full-time education in the year of their third birthday), public funding and quality standards (pre-school 3–6 professionals have the same requirements as elementary school teachers). As a result, Spain and Italy perform above European averages in Early Years Education provision for children aged three (or two-and-a-half) and older.

Childcare provision for children under three has, however, had a totally different fate. Institutional support and public funding have been considerably weaker and as a result coverage is much lower, the degree of territorial fragmentation higher and the role of private (for profit) provision much stronger. During the years of rapid economic growth and massive entrance of women into the labour market (from the mid-1990s until the outbreak of the financial crisis and the bursting of the housing bubble), enrolment rates increased. Both conservative and socialist central governments as well as regional governments increased funding. However, this expansion was not substantially matched by an improvement in quality standards, nor did it prevent the private sector from increasing its presence; quite the opposite in fact. Over the past decade, some regions have externalised their provision (i.e. municipal nurseries privately managed) to a large extent and this has had negative consequences for the working conditions of staff, for whom the main direct or indirect reference for salary setting is the minimum wage, which often functions as a real wage floor, and, thus, as happens in low-paid and weakly unionised sectors, their situation is strongly shaped by a dualised and fragmented labour market (Ibáñez & León 2014b).

As regards family policies oriented towards the reconciliation of work and family life, important pieces of legislation have been introduced since the end of the 1990s. In 1999, Aznar's government approved the first national law on work/life balance, which improved maternity and paternity leave and regulated time off work to care for dependent relatives and small children. In 2003, the conservative government also introduced the National Plan for Family Support. Two of the most important measures implemented were financial support for working mothers with children under the age of three (€1,200 per year per child) and a subsidy to firms that employed women (León & Salido 2012). The proof of success of these new measures introduced by the Partido Popular (PP) government is their continuity under the succeeding centre-left government of Zapatero, which added a third one-off payment of €2,500 for the birth or adoption of a child. Both gender equality legislation and family policies were firmly promoted in the years immediately preceding the economic crisis under the two socialist governments (2004–08 and 2008–11). As a first gesture towards feminism, Prime Minister Zapatero formed the first gender parity government in Spanish history in April 2004. Gender equality institutional bodies were given the highest ranks within the central administration (Bustelo & Ortbals 2007). During this period the government passed a number of important pro-gender-equality laws such as Law 13/2005 on same-sex marriage (which included the right to adoption and paternity for same-sex couples). Other important gender equality measures introduced in the first mandate of Zapatero's government were, firstly, the 2004 Law on Gender Violence and, secondly, the 2007 law for the promotion of effective equality between women and men. This gender equality law had a wide scope of action. In relation to family policies the most significant aspect of the law was an improvement in parental and maternity leave, especially for the most vulnerable groups. The new norm granted statutory maternity leave for women under 21 years of age, the equality law had a wide scop and those with no right to contributory benefit. It also increased the length of fathers' leave to 13 days at 100 per cent of salary. The law stipulated that this 'daddy' quota would progressively increase to reach four months of remunerated leave in 2013. However, as we will later see, these provisions were stopped in the first austerity package introduced in 2010 and have been on hold until now.

The pre-crisis decade also witnessed the creation of a national law for long-term care. The *Ley de Dependencia* was introduced in 2006 (Act 39/2006) by the Partido Socialista Obrero Español (PSOE) government. This new norm established for the first time a universal right to long-term care for individuals with reduced autonomy. Within the framework of the Spanish welfare state, the Dependency law is indeed a clear departure from an institutional tradition where invalidity and retirement pensions were almost the only form of public protection for the elderly and where social services usually had a means-tested (non-universal) character. However, the actual implementation of the new system has been riddled with difficulties. Insufficient and unclear financing, tensions between different levels of government and a lack of realistic assessment of available resources have resulted in weak implementation (León 2011). Although the *Ley de Dependencia* had a 'social-democratic' spirit in that it aimed to provide universal long-term care services, in reality it has been widely used as a conditional cash-for-care programme (by February 2011, 65 per cent of public expenditure on long-term care went to cash allowances [SAAD/IMSERSO 2011]). According to recent research, more than half of these cash allowances are used either totally or partially to employ a care worker in the home, often one of migrant origin (CASER 2009). Thus, despite a progressive piece of legislation, and a considerable increase in public spending, long-term care continues to be provided by families with a substantial contribution from private markets and migrant work. In fact, the role of migrant care work has been tolerated if not encouraged at an institutional level in several ways. In the regularisation process of 2005, 83 per cent of applicants were granted work permits (over half a million people), of whom one-third applied through the domestic sector. This boosted the number of migrant workers registered under the special social security regime of registered household employees (León 2011). As in Italy, then, long term care policies, labour market regulations and migration policies have intertwined to shape in specific and 'southern' ways the development of this care market (Ranci & Sabatinelli, 2014; Ibáñez & León 2014a).

Trends on expenditure bear witness to these changes over time for the two countries. As Table 1 shows, Spain started in 2000 from a relatively low level of per-capita expenditure in family/children policies (38.2 per cent of the European Union [EU]-15 average). In 2007 the situation had strongly improved (the per-capita expenditure was 54.8 per cent of the Western European average). However, with the onset of the crisis this process of narrowing the distance with Western Europe has reversed, as the data relating to 2011 show (51.3 per cent of the EU-15 average). As for Italy, this country spent around 45 per cent of the Western European average in 2000 and it reduced its distance from the EU-15 countries at a slower pace than Spain. Both countries in 2007 had reached a similar distance from the rest of Western Europe.

With the onset of the crisis, Spain started to cut expenditure in real terms ($-0.3$ per cent on a yearly average between 2007 and 2011), whereas Italy substantially froze expenditure growth ($+0.6$ per cent).

These data help us also to frame under a clearer light the trends in Spain and Italy. Both countries were lagging behind the rest of Western Europe, with Spain even further away than Italy: in terms of expenditure what we have witnessed in the last decade is a shortening of distances not only between Spain and the EU-15 countries, but also between the former and Italy.

**Table 1** Family and Children Expenditure in Spain, Italy and Western Europe over Time (2000–11)

| | Euro per inhabitant (at constant 2005 prices) | | | | | Purchasing Power Standard per inhabitant EU-15 = 100 | | |
|---|---|---|---|---|---|---|---|---|
| | 2000 | 2007 | 2011 | yearly variation percentage 2000–07 | yearly variation percentage 2007–11 | 2000 | 2007 | 2011 |
| EU-15 | 536.7 | 583.8 | 613.4 | +1.3 | +1.3 | 100.0 | 100.0 | 100.0 |
| Spain | 178.4 | 273.1 | 270.0 | +7.6 | −0.3 | 38.2 | 54.8 | 51.3 |
| Italy | 245.0 | 310.5 | 317.7 | +3.8 | 0.6 | 44.8 | 54.3 | 55.8 |

*Source:* Eurostat European System of Integrated Social Protection Statistics (ESSPROSS) database (2014).

**Table 2** Changes in Care Coverage over Time: Italy and Spain in a Comparative Perspective

| | Expenditure on elderly care as a percentage of GDP[a] | | Childcare coverage[b] (percentage on <3 year old population) | |
|---|---|---|---|---|
| | 1994 | 2008 | 2005 | 2012 |
| Spain | 0.17 | 0.45 | 39 | 36 |
| Italy | 0.12 | 0.14 | 25 | 20 |

*Source:* Eurostat.
*Notes:* [a]ESSPROSS database (2014); [b]EU-SILC database.

Also the data in Table 2 seem to support the idea that there has been a different dynamic of investment in elderly care and childcare in the two countries.

The following section looks at factors that may have the capacity to explain the scope for policy recalibration and/or retrenchment in the domain of family and care policies in the two countries. As will be shown, these factors have had different weight in the two countries in either facilitating or hindering policy change. The section follows to some degree Da Roit and Sabatinelli's (2013) article on recent developments on childcare and eldercare policies in Italy.

## Some Potential Explanations for the Diverging Paths before the Crisis

To begin with, and as already argued, Spain's more pronounced dynamics of innovation in the last two decades can be interpreted as a catching up process in comparison with Italy. But we need broader explanations to interpret, firstly, the scope of the changes in terms of policy inputs in the two countries and, secondly, the 'resilience' of some of these innovative social policies with the outbreak of the crisis. Table 3 offers a comparison between Italy and Spain on a series of dimensions. The upper part of the table focuses more on cultural and structural facets of the two countries during the decade preceding the economic crisis of 2008. In particular, Spain and Italy are compared in terms of cultural values and value changes in relation to family issues over the recent decades. Then financial constraints are taken into consideration, as well as welfare policy legacies (both in relation to the main pillar of 'old risks' protection, the pensions system and family care policies). The structure of the labour market and in particular the institutional regulation of low-skilled occupations in the service sector has also been examined.

An element that distinguishes Spain from Italy is how cultural and social values have changed in recent years. The Spanish more proactive path of reform towards the institutional delegitimation of the traditional male-breadwinner model compared with Italy seems in line with a clearer departure from ideas regarding the traditional division of paid and unpaid labour and more conservative attitudes regarding gender roles. In this respect, the shift towards the dual worker model seems to have been significant in Spain. From similar (low) levels at the beginning of the 1990s

**Table 3** Italy and Spain: A Comparative View of Differences and Similarities of Potential Factors Affecting Policy Change

| Factors affecting policy change | Italy | Spain |
|---|---|---|
| *Cultural values and value changes in relation to family issues over the last two decades:* | Slow modernisation and still strong traditional familistic values | Modernisation and partial overcoming of traditional familistic values; strong secularisation |
| *Financial constraints* | | |
| Average debt/GDP ratio (1997–2007) | 121.5% | 59.7% |
| Average yearly deficit (as percentage of GDP) (1997–2007) | 2.9% | 0.5% |
| *Policy legacy* | | |
| Relevance of old age pensions expenditure; average yearly incidence on: | The 'Pension State' | Not a 'Pension State' (in line with other EU-15 countries) |
| GDP (1997–2007) | 12.4% | 7.0% |
| total government expenditure (1997–2007) | 26.0% | 17.9% |
| total social protection expenditure (1997–2007) | 50.0% | 34.8% |
| *Strength of previous welfare programmes in the 1990s in the following family policy fields* | | |
| Childcare | Limited Diffusion | Limited Diffusion |
| Long-term care | Relevant cash programme (CA) | Limited (social assistance) |
| *Functioning of the labour market and its institutional regulation:* | Acceptance of 'grey' markets in the low-skilled service sector. Dual labour market | Acceptance of 'grey' markets in the low-skilled service sector Dual labour market |

(around 20 percentage points lower than other European countries), the evolution of female activity in the labour market in Spain from the mid-1990s and until the end of economic expansion in 2008 contributed to narrowing the gap in relation to EU average figures, especially for the younger generations (León & Migliavacca 2013). With regard to ideals about motherhood and parenthood, according to the most recent waves of the European Value Studies, while in Italy the view that a mother's work is potentially harmful to child development is the predominant opinion across all cohorts, in Spain the percentage of respondents in agreement is much lower with a very significant generation gap (60 per cent of the 25–49 cohort are in disagreement with the statement). Similarly, agreement with the capacity of fathers to look after children is higher among Spaniards, especially the young, than among Italians (Naldini & Jurado 2013). These changes in attitudes also correlate with diverging patterns in family dynamics. The higher incidence of cohabitation, non-marital births and divorce over the last two decades signals a weaker incidence of the Catholic Church in shaping family-related issues in Spain than in Italy (Moreno & Marí-Klose 2014).

At a first level of analysis one could deduct that in the Spanish case the changes in attitudes and behaviours accelerated the need for a less traditional and more egalitarian approach to family policies, while in the Italian case the pressure has been less evident.

A second relevant factor affecting the divergence in reform paths has to do with financial constraints. If we look at the decade before the crisis (1997–2007), the average ratio between public debt and gross domestic product (GDP) was around 120 per cent, whereas in the same years it was approximately 60 per cent in the EU as a whole and in Spain in particular. Moreover, Italy was a country with one of the highest mean annual deficits in the same years (around three per cent of GDP). Such a situation has strongly limited the space for innovation and for expanding policy fields such as family policies. In Spain, by contrast, the average yearly deficit in the same decade was approximately 0.5 per cent.

A third important element has to do with potential path dependence and policy legacy mechanisms (Pierson 1998). Italy and Spain differ strongly in relation to the centrality of the most traditional pillar of social protection: old age pensions. Italy, even after the reforms of the 1990s, has remained a 'Pensions State' (Fargion 2009; Hinricks & Jessoula 2012): old age pensions represented more than 12 per cent of GDP, 26 per cent of total government expenditure and accounted for half of total social protection expenditure in the decade 1997–2007. These features made Italy an almost unique case in Western Europe in terms of the centrality of the pensions system in the Welfare State. Spain, instead looks less like an outlier in European context with a less pronounced role played by pensions in social protection and, more generally, in government expenditure. Considering pensions is important because this has been one of the main fields where social and political stakeholders have confronted each other in recent decades. A social policy arena focused on pension reforms, where pensions are the main pillar of the welfare state (Italy), could develop dynamics of change quite different from another policy arena where pensions are not as central (Spain) (Bonoli & Natali 2012).

If we look at policy legacy in family policies until the mid-1990s, we see fewer differences in the two countries in terms of diffusion of services. Both countries have had the capacity to innovate and expand high quality services with the integration of the pre-school years as the first non-compulsory stage of elementary education. For both Italy and Spain the development of 'infant schools' under the auspices of education instead of welfare services constitutes the only robust evidence of social investment. However, childcare for children under the age of three has had weaker institutional support and the scope for expansion has remained small. Long-term care in Italy was based on a national universalistic programme (the Companion Allowance), providing only cash allowances of a limited per-capita amount, but still offered to about five to seven per cent of the elderly population. In Spain, instead, prior to the Dependency Law there were only local assistance schemes, covering the frail elderly most in need. In Italian long-term care there has therefore been a programme, with a constituency and a moderate coverage level, that has to be taken into consideration when we look at reforms, because it represented both a first answer (insufficient but relevant) to long-term care needs and it created a constituency, scared that reforms could harm its rights to access care.

If we look at how the Italian and Spanish labour market have been working, there has been a partial acceptance of 'grey', irregular markets, especially in those occupations connected to domestic work (Bettio et al. 2012). Furthermore, a strong tendency towards the dualisation of the labour market has been present in both countries. This strong segmentation affects both the need for family policies for the more vulnerable groups as well as the redistributive capacity of family policies. Spain is an extreme case in the European context in the incidence of temporary work that has a clear precarious character (Polavieja 2006). Labour market reforms over the last three decades have, whether purposely or not, resulted in a deepening of the two-tier system of protected versus unprotected workers. The poor working conditions of 'outsiders' in the Italian and Spanish markets turn into poor social protection with a high risk of unemployment, which is especially acute in Spain. The lack of minimum income schemes and/or comprehensive unemployment assistance means that many workers in and out of employment are forced to rely on family or social assistance support (Malo 2011; Marx & Picot 2014). Family policies do not seem to offer any alternative route of social protection to those who fall outside unemployment schemes in any of the two countries.

## The Effects of the Crisis on Family Policies in Italy and Spain

Despite laudable pre-crisis attempts in the Spanish case to depart from its familistic imprint, the sequence of events post-2008 indicates that Spain has not been able to live up to expectations. The abrupt 'end of the illusion' that came after 2008 with the outbreak of the global financial crisis and the bursting of the housing bubble brought high unemployment, social unrest and massive social expenditure cuts. The conservative government elected in 2011 is also implementing changes of a more ideological nature that undermine much of the progressive character of legislation introduced by previous governments. Although a longer time span will be needed to truly assess the effects of the economic crisis on the welfare systems of Italy and Spain, initial evaluations indicate that the financial crisis and the austerity programmes that followed served in a way to level the playing field between the two (Pavolini et al. 2014).

The effect that the financial crisis has had and is having on the economies, institutions and societies of the countries of Southern Europe has already attracted considerable academic attention. Especially since 2010, the degree of international 'intrusiveness' - meaning strong pressure exercised by the European Commission, the International Monetary Fund and the European Central Bank on national governments with a high deficit problem – has led to strong across-the-board cuts in public spending. Universalistic and residual welfare programmes have become a rapid saving formula even if the consequences of the crisis, especially for unemployment, will require an increase, not the opposite, in these policy domains.

In Italy, the recent budget-planning laws (especially those in 2010–12) deliberated quite draconian expenditure cuts. For example, since 2008 the national government has cut expenditure on a series of funds. The main social fund used to finance local authorities for social care services was reduced by 92 per cent in the years 2007–12 (Basile 2011).

A broader change in social care and social assistance in terms of retrenchment could come from the laws approved by the Berlusconi government between July and September 2011, whereby it was decided to cut expenditure in the following years. Among the types of provision at risk of elimination or reduction are deductions for the costs of care for dependent people, and care allowances. Already more recent national data have started to confirm this trend: between 2009 and 2012 social care and social assistance expenditure dropped by 3.5 per cent (Istat 2013).

The last few years, when the crisis and austerity have set in, have witnessed a continuation to what has happened previously with only one main change. The institutional inertia at a national level has turned into retrenchment and it has been matched by a weakening of the 'modernisation from below' process. Such cuts have put even more pressure on local stakeholders at a time when the weaknesses of the financial basis of their action had become clearly apparent. Facing a central government that was cutting down transfers and with a crisis in their own revenues, many local authorities have had to reduce or to reconsider their capacity to deliver care services. Often the answer has not been to cut services but to raise co-payments and fees. At the same time many households are facing a deep labour market crisis, with rising unemployment rates, which make it difficult even for many middle class families to have enough private resources to access the private care market. Enterprises are also more often in dire straits and offering care services is becoming for many a luxury they cannot afford.

In Spain, the outbreak of the crisis in 2008 has to a large extent limited the reach of the new measures introduced during the period of economic growth, with path dependency dynamics becoming more obvious. From 2010 onwards (absolute majority of PP since November 2011) gender equality policies and family policies have been subject to drastic cuts. Institutions and government bodies created to promote gender equality have either been dismantled or downgraded. As for actual policies, the economic crisis and the austerity measures implemented as a unique exit formula have hindered their continuity. This is the case with the paternity benefit that the 2007 Equality Act provided for; its implementation has not yet taken place. The most recent labour market reform (Law 3/2012, 6 July) also curtailed rights to time off work for work/family balance reasons. It also introduced the possibility of extra hours for part-time employment (this was not allowed before), in reality increasing the availability of part-time workers to employer demand.

Cuts have also been severe in childcare and long-term care. In the 2012 budget, financial investment in the Educa3 programme (childcare for children under the age of three) and the long-term care system has been discontinued. The implementation of the Dependency law has also been jeopardised by budgetary cuts that in 2011 amounted to 5.2 per cent, which is even more problematic considering that the Law was born without a tax earmarked to secure its proper financing. The budgets of the regions have also been drastically cut for the sake of stability, which is forcing them to also make cuts in minimum income and social exclusion programmes. In both cases, childcare and care of dependent elderly, the pendulum has swung back to assistentialism. It is interesting to note that a partial reaction to the freeze and cuts of the national governments has been a sort of modernisation from below, as took place in Italy in the previous decade. To the quasi-institutional paralysis at a time when social demand is at its highest levels (due to very high unemployment and an upsurge in poverty levels especially among households with small children) non-state parties are taking action and claiming space in the public arena. From organised social movements to community action, we see a myriad of interventions taking place primarily outside the scope of state action. In many senses, some of these interventions are renovating and reconfiguring old familistic practices. This process which also correlates with the eruption of new forces in the political arena will surely become an interesting focus for further research.

## Conclusions

Centring our analysis on family and care policies, we have argued in this paper that the policy trajectories of Italy and Spain differed during the 1990s and the 2000s mainly at a nominal level, given a strong catching up impulse towards greater European convergence in the Spanish case which led to unprecedented legislation and policy. In Italy, since the turn of the century, reforms have borne mainly a retrenchment impact on the overall functioning of the welfare state, while in Spain the scope for innovation has been leading towards a more sustained recalibration process. Importantly, though, this alleged path departure in the case of Spain decreases when the focus is on the long-term prospects of this trajectory and its effects on some of the more pressing social problems. Whilst higher fiscal constraints, a more traditional familistic culture and the greater path dependency of the 'pension state' have hindered the capacity for policy change in Italy to a greater extent than in Spain, in both countries a highly dualised labour market, the absence of minimum protection schemes, and the marginal role that family and care policies play in the overall design of the welfare states are factors that continue to influence the capacity of both countries to respond to persistent social problems. For both Italy and Spain, the only clear example of a policy domain framed under the social investment logic is the organisation of three years of pre-school within the education system although this was something that was introduced some time ago (1968 in Italy and 1990 in Spain).

The economic crisis (with both external and internal dynamics) has placed both countries in a phase of 'permanent strain', dominated by social expenditure cuts and other austerity programmes. In more recent years, social innovation from below rather than social investment from the top has come to the fore as new form of organised collective action worth noting.

## References

Andreotti, A., Mingione, E. & Polizzi, E. (2012) 'Local welfare systems: a challenge for social cohesion', *Urban Studies*, vol. 49, no. 9, pp. 1925–1940.

Ascoli, U. & Pavolini, E. (2012) 'Ombre rosse. il sistema di welfare italiano dopo venti anni di riforme', *Stato e Mercato*, vol. 96, pp. 429–464.

Basile, R. (2011) 'Tagli al welfare. C'è un futuro per le politiche sociali?', *Rivista delle Politiche Sociali*, vol. 3, pp. 543–558.

Bettio, F., Corsi, M., D'Ippoliti, F., Lyberaki, A., Samek Lodovici, M. & Verashchagina, A. (2012) *The Impact of the Economic Crisis on the Situation of Women and Men and on Gender Equality Policies*, European Commission, Brussels.

Bonoli, G. & Natali, D. (eds) (2012) *The Politics of the New Welfare State*, Oxford University Press, Oxford.

Bustelo, M. & Ortbals, C. (2007) 'The evolution of Spanish state feminism. A fragmented landscape', in *Changing State Feminism*, eds J. Outshoorn & J. Kantola, Basingstoke, Palgrave, pp. 201–223.

CASER (Fundación para la Dependencia). (2009) 'Ayudas a la dependencia en España. Situación actual', available on line at: http://www.fundacioncaser.es

Costa, G. (2012) 'Long-term care Italian policies: a case of inertial institutional change', in *Long-term Policy Reforms in Europe*, eds C. Ranci & E. Pavolini, Springer, New York, pp. 103–124.

Da Roit, B. & Sabatinelli, S. (2013) 'Nothing on the move or just going private? Understanding the freeze on child- and eldercare policies and the development of care markets in Italy', *Social Politics: International Studies in Gender, State & Society*, vol. 20, no. 3, pp. 430–453.

Esping-Andersen, G. (1999) *Social Foundations of Postindustrial Economies*, Oxford University Press, Oxford.

Fargion, V. (2009) 'Italy: still a pension state?', in *International Social Policy*, eds P. Alcock & G. Craig, Basingstoke, Palgrave, pp. 171–194.

Ferrera, M. (1996) 'The Southern model of welfare in Social Europe', *Journal of European Social Policy*, vol. 6, no. 1, pp. 17–37.

Ferrera, M., Hemerijck, A. & Rhodes, M. (2000) *The Future of Social Europe: Recasting Work and Welfare in the New Economy*, Celta Editora, Oeiras.

Flaquer, L. (2000) *Las Políticas Familares en una Perspectiva Comparada* Colección Estudios Sociales Núm. 3, Fundación La Caixa, available online at: http://bit.ly/1qjuBWH

Guillén, A. M. & León, M. (eds) (2011) *The Spanish Welfare State in European Context*, Ashgate, Farnham.

Guillén, A. M. (2010) 'Defrosting the Spanish welfare state: The weight of conservative components', in *A Long Good–Bye to Bismarck: The Politics of Welfare Reforms in Continental Welfare States*, ed. B. Palier, Amsterdam University Press, Amsterdam, pp. 183–206.

Hinrichs, K. & Jessoula, M. (eds) (2012) *Labour Market Flexibility and Pension Reforms. Flexible Today, Secure Tomorrow?* Palgrave, Basingstoke.

Ibáñez, Z. & León, M. (2014a) 'Resisting crisis at what cost? Migrant care workers in private households', in *Care and Migrant Labour: Theory, Policy and Politics*, eds B. Anderson & I. Shutes, Palgrave, Basingstoke (*forthcoming*).

Ibáñez, Z. & d León, M. (2014b) 'Early childhood education and care provision in Spain', in *The Transformation of Care in European Societies*, ed. M. León, Palgrave, Basingstoke (*forthcoming*).

Istat (2013) *La spesa sociale dei Comuni. Anno 2011*, Istat, Rome.

Kazepov, Y. (ed) (2010) *Rescaling Social Policies Toward Multilevel Governance in Europe*, Ashgate, Farnham.

Keck, W. & Saraceno, C. (2010) 'Can we identify intergenerational policy regimes in Europe?', *European Societies*, vol. 12, no. 5, pp. 675–696.

León, M. (2002) 'Towards the individualization of social rights: hidden familialistic practices in Spanish social policy', *South European Society and Politics*, vol. 7, no. 3, pp. 53–80.

León, M. (2011) 'The quest for gender equality', in *The Spanish Welfare State in the European Context*, eds A. Guillén & M. León, Ashgate, Farnham, pp. 59–74.

León, M. & Migliavacca, M. (2013) 'Italy and Spain: still the case of familistic welfare models?', *Population Review*, vol. 25, no. 1, pp. 25–42.

León, M. & Salido, O. (2012) 'Políticas de conciliación entre la vida familiar y la laboral', in *Transformaciones del Estado de Bienestar en perspectiva comparada*, eds E. Del Pino & J. Rubio, Editorial Tecnos, Madrid, pp. 291–309.

Maino, F. & Neri, S. (2011) 'Explaining welfare reforms in Italy between economy and politics: external constraints and endogenous dynamics', *Social Policy & Administration*, vol. 45, no. 4, pp. 445–464.

Malo, M. Á. (2011) *Labour Market Policies in Spain under the Current Recession*, International Labour Organisation, Geneva, available online at: http://bit.ly/1ly76D5

Marx, P. & Picot, G. (2014) 'Labour market policies and party preferences of fixed-term workers', in *How Welfare States Shape the Democratic Public: Policy Feedback, Participation, Voting, and Attitudes*, eds S. Kumlin & I. Stadelmann-Steffen, Edward Elgar, Cheltenham, pp. 112–130.

Morel, N., Palier, B. & Palme, J. (eds) (2012) *Towards a Social Investment Welfare State? Ideas, Policies and Challenges*, Policy Press, Bristol.

Moreno, L. (2001) *La vía media española del modelo de bienestar mediterráneo*, CSIC, Madrid.

Moreno, L. & Marí-Klose, P. (2014) 'Youth, family change and welfare arrangements', *Is the South so different?*, *European Societies*, vol. 15, no. 4, pp. 493–513.

Naldini, M. & Jurado, T. (2013) 'Family and welfare wtate reorientation in Spain and inertia in Italy from a European Perspective', *Population Review*, vol. 52, no. 1, pp. 343–353.

Naldini, M. & Saraceno, C. (2008) 'Social and family policies in Italy: not totally frozen but far from structural reforms', *Social Policy & Administration*, vol. 42, no. 7, pp. 733–748.

Pavolini, E., Ascoli, U. & Mirabile, M. L. (2013) *Tempi moderni. Il welfare nelle imprese in Italia*, Il Mulino, Bologna.

Pavolini, E., León, M., Guillén, A. M. & d Ascoli, U. (2014) 'From austerity to permanent strain? The EU and welfare state reform in Italy and Spain', *Comparative European Politics* (*forthcoming*).

Pfau-Effinger, B. (1998) 'Gender cultures and the gender arrangement – a theoretical framework for cross-national comparisons on gender', *The European Journal of Social Sciences*, vol. 11, no. 2, pp. 147–166.

Pierson, P. (1998) 'Irresistible forces, immovable objects: post-industrial welfare states confront permanent austerity', *Journal of European Public Policy*, vol. 5, no. 4, pp. 539–560.

Polavieja, J. G. (2006) 'The incidence of temporary employment in advanced economies: why is Spain different?', *European Sociological Review*, vol. 22, no. 1, pp. 61–78.

Ranci, C. & Sabatinelli, S. (2014) 'Long term and child care policies in Italy between familism and privatisation', in *The Transformation of Care in European Societies*, ed. M. León, Palgrave, Basingstoke (*forthcoming*).

SAAD/IMSERSO (Sistema para la Autonomía y Atención a la Dependencia/Instituto de Mayores y Servicios Sociales). (2011) 'Estadísticas del sistema para la autonomía y la atención a la dependencia. Situación a 1 de Febrero 2011', available online at: http://www.imsersomayores. csic.es

Sabatinelli, S. (ed) (2010) *Le politiche per i bambini in età prescolare in Italia e in Europa*, QUID IRS, Milano.

Valiente, C. (1996) 'Family obligations in Spain', in *Family Obligations in Europe*, eds J. Millar & A. Warman, Family Policy Studies Centre, London, pp. 325–358.

Valiente, C. (2013) 'Gender equality policymaking in Spain (2008–11): losing momentum', in *Politics and Society in Contemporary Spain: From Zapatero to Rajoy*, eds B. N. Field & A. Botti, Basingstoke, Palgrave, pp. 179–195.

# Welfare Performance in Southern Europe: Employment Crisis and Poverty Risk

Rodolfo Gutiérrez

*The Great Recession has had a deep impact on employment levels and on income inequality in the Southern European countries (Greece, Spain, Portugal and Italy). It has given rise to a new stage in the discussion on the distinctiveness of a possible 'Mediterranean' variant of welfare capitalism. This paper analyses the performance of the Mediterranean cluster during the Great Recession period in its two main dimensions, labour market participation and poverty risk, and to what extent that performance has evolved in a divergent or convergent manner. Firstly, it portrays the main changes in this variant of welfare capitalism during the last two decades. The second and third sections, respectively, provide a comparative profile of the employment crisis suffered by these countries and of its impact on poverty risks. Finally, the main institutional traits are discussed, explaining the relative performance of welfare capitalism in this cluster of countries.*

The Great Recession has had a deep impact on employment levels and on income inequality in the Southern European (SE) countries (Greece, Spain, Portugal and Italy). These four countries lost six million paid jobs between 2007 and 2013. The two countries that have most suffered from the employment crisis, Greece and Spain, have lost almost one job out of five. In Portugal, the loss has been lower, around 13 per cent and in Italy it has been notably lower, with a drop in employment of only 4.5 per cent. The crisis has also resulted in a sudden increase in pressure on social expenditure, but income inequality and poverty risk levels have increased in the four countries. Social expenditure in percentage of gross domestic product (GDP) rocketed during the first years of the crisis and has become more stable in recent years. In Greece and Spain it has risen to a great extent, as expenditure went from 20.8 per cent in 2007 to 26.1 per cent in 2011 and from 24.3 to 30.2, respectively. In Portugal it rose from 23.9 to 26.5; and in Italy from 26.6 to 29.7.

Participation in employment and the capacity to reduce the inequality of incomes are the two most crucial dimensions of the performance of welfare capitalism. The magnitude of the crisis in these two dimensions has provided the worst image of the performance of the Mediterranean model. However, it was assumed that in the last two decades these countries had carried out processes of modernisation and recalibration of their welfare systems which had allowed them to improve their performance in these two dimensions and reduce the weakness that was attributed to them in the initial characterisation of this cluster of welfare systems, at the start of the 1990s. The enormous impact of the crisis in these countries has not only revived concerns about whether they had effectively carried out improvements in their welfare system as was supposed, but also reinforced the idea that these countries differed little from each other in this performance and continued to share the main characteristic of very weak welfare capitalism.

This paper analyses the performance of Mediterranean welfare capitalism during the Great Recession period in its two main dimensions, labour market participation and poverty risk, and to what extent that performance has evolved in a divergent or convergent manner. Firstly, the main changes in this variant of welfare capitalism during the last two decades are portrayed. In the second and third sections, respectively, a comparative profile is provided of the employment crisis suffered by these countries and of its impact on poverty risks. Finally, the main institutional traits are discussed, explaining the relative performance of welfare capitalism in this cluster of countries.

## Welfare Capitalism in Southern Europe: Recalibration and Performance

The Great Recession has given rise to a new stage in the discussion on the distinctiveness of a possible 'Mediterranean' variant of welfare capitalism (Ferrera 1996; 2005; Petmesidou & Papatheodorou 2006). With some differences in timing, the expansion of welfare provision in this cluster of countries between the 1960s and the 1980s displayed certain similarities, founded on a shared cultural heritage and similar dynamics of a more recent and compressed process of social modernisation. Mediterranean countries showed a peak of commonalities in the early 1990s in all of the three 'pillars' of welfare provision. The Mediterranean labour market exhibited three main traits: the predominance of the male as the major household breadwinner, a low and secondary labour participation of young people of both genders and of adult women, and some form of 'insider/outsider' dualism induced by a high level of employment protection and a weak level of unemployment. Four main traits characterised the Mediterranean welfare state: the low redistributive effect of social transfers and taxes; the bias of the social transfer system towards the risks of elderly people as opposed to the risks of infancy and youth; and the high levels of poverty risks, associated with poor development of minimum income schemes. In the third pillar, the strong reliance on the family for the provision of basic economic security and care for its members has had the function of legitimating both low provision of social services and low demand to reduce labour market dualism.

In the second half of the 1990s, that relative balance of Mediterranean welfare systems began to receive a series of internal and external pressures that gave rise to a new phase in its development. The greater opening up to global competition of their economies and the process of Europeanisation on the external front, as well as the post-industrial transition with its deployment of new social risks, policies of fiscal balance, and political-administrative decentralisation on the domestic front, resulted in a phase of ambitious welfare modernisation and recalibration (Guillén & Matsaganis 2000; Ferrera & Hemerijck 2003; Hemerijck 2013). The four countries shared some ingredients of this recalibration which affected the 'traditional balance': reduction of generous guarantees for privileged occupational groups, accompanied by the improvement of a minimum of social benefits; the expansion and amelioration of family benefits and social services, with more attention to gender equality and labour market reforms with the goal of reducing segmentation and insider protection.

At this stage, Italy is the country that goes through a recalibration in more dimensions of welfare (Ferrera & Gaulmini 2000; Sachi & Bastagli 2005, Jessoula & Alti 2010). The objective of stopping the expansion of a hypertrophic pension system has been key to these changes. Its successive reforms, although of a different nature in several aspects, have gone in the direction of balancing the rights of different occupational groups, with improvements of the lowest pensions and new access rights for atypical workers. Some traditional deficits in social coverage were filled, but social assistance and social services are mainly in the hands of fairly weak local and regional governments, providing a wide range of targeted programmes with a very high variation in access regulation and generosity.

In Spain, from the mid-1980s important changes were carried out in welfare: adopting a national health system, ensuring universal access to education and pensions and establishing minimum income programmes at a regional level (Guillén 2010; Guillén & León 2011). Pensions and unemployment insurance continued to be funded by social contributions, while other non-contributory and social assistance benefits would be financed by taxation. At the start of the new millennium, the system was enriched with two new additions: firstly, a new social assistance scheme, the Renta Activa de Inserción (RAI)/Active Integration Income, aimed at those aged 45 and over who have exhausted their unemployment benefits and have family dependents; and, secondly, a law to provide public services and benefits to care for dependent people. To this, an intense process of decentralisation of responsibilities in the welfare services was added, both in health and in education and social services, leading to a widespread expansion of those services and also increasing signs of inequalities between regions, mainly in the provision of social services (Cabrero 2011). Also in the first part of this decade, changes were carried out towards relaxing the protection of insiders and improving the social protection of temporary workers. Although the recalibration of the Spanish system has been notable, expanding social assistance and minimum income protection, its basic two-tier architecture has largely remained since the mid-2000s, with a generous social insurance system for core workers and only meagre protection, in both employment protection and unemployment insurance, for secondary workers, mainly young, low-qualified temporary workers and the long-term unemployed (Mato 2011).

In Portugal, the reforms of this period, led by socialist governments in 1995–2002 and 2005–2011, meant an expansion of social protection (Guillén, Álvarez & Adão E. Silva 2003; Capucha et al. 2005). A national minimum income system was adopted in 1997. In a reorientation of reforms towards goals of job creation, improvements in unemployment security were introduced and programmes of occupational training and insertion were set up, as well as incentives to mobilise local potential for the creation of employment. The pension system underwent a major reform in 2006, which incorporated a sustainability factor to link benefits to life expectancy.

Greece has been the country of this group in which the results of recalibration have been less (Matsaganis 2005; Spanou & Sotiropoulos 2011). After the country joined the European Union (EU), reforms were adopted towards expanding universal coverage of the health care system and the extension of social assistance to new groups. However, the reforms of this period have failed to overcome the two major problems in the development of the Greek welfare system: on the one hand, welfare provision aimed at a great variety of interest groups, which reinforced the institutional fragmentation and clientelist practice of the state, and, on the other, partially due to this fragmentation, the failure to tackle the unequal and unsustainable pension system. In such conditions of institutional fragmentation and weakness of the state, attempts to build a safety net covering the many social welfare deficits produced no substantial reforms.

Under the dual influence of European integration and globalisation of their economies, the four countries of SE had gradually caught up with the wealthiest European countries by the mid-2000s. They have undergone similar processes of recalibration of their welfare states and attempts to achieve a less dualistic labour market, which, with different intensities and nuances in each country, took away some of the singularity of the Mediterranean variant of welfare capitalism (Karamessini 2008; Ferrera 2010; Mari-Klose & Moreno-Fuentes 2013). Portugal and Spain, with better institutional capabilities supported by social pacts, were more successful than Italy and Greece in their functional recalibration efforts, and they were able to establish less dualistic and more internally homogeneous social insurance systems and also a more effective and inclusive safety net. In terms of distributive recalibration, with the exception of Greece, SE countries reduced their insider-biased welfare, although the path of reform in this dimension has been slow and only partially successful.

In the central part of the economic growth cycle, although unevenly, these countries gradually reduced the difference in social expenditure from the EU average. In 2007, Italy almost equalled in percentage of social expenditure of the GDP, at 26.6 per cent, the average of the euro countries (EU-17), 26.9 per cent; Greece and Portugal drew closer, with 24.8 and 23.9 per cent, respectively; and Spain was further away with 20.8 per cent. The distance was slightly greater in social expenditure per capita: Italy's annual spending of euros per capita (in Purchasing Power Standard) was 92.2 per cent of that of the EU-17 (eurozone) while the corresponding figures for the other SE countries were: Greece 76.1, Spain 72.2 and Portugal 62.5.

The differences in the functional composition of social expenditure were even more pronounced in these countries, showing the uneven results of the recalibration process. Italy very prominently, but also Greece and Portugal, continued to offer welfare provision with a certain old-age bias: in 2007, while the whole of the EU-17 spent on that function 38.8 per cent of their total social expenditure, Italy spent 51.6, Greece 43.6 and Portugal 42.9; Spain had reduced it to 33.2. The singularity in the composition of Italian welfare was confirmed with its low allocation of expenditure to the other two functions aimed at the most common social risks in the central stages of the life cycle: unemployment and the protection of families and children. In 2007 Italy spent only 1.7 per cent on unemployment protection – compared with 10.1 per cent for Spain and a level around the eurozone average, and in the region of five per cent for Greece and Portugal – although it had a similar level of unemployment to the EU-17, but with generous unemployment insurance and a rather higher level of rotation between employment and unemployment. Italy also had the lowest allocation of social expenditure both on family/children and on social exclusion benefits: 5.1 per cent, roughly half of the 9.7 per cent in the EU-17, and lower than in Greece (8.5), Spain (7.4) and Portugal (6.5).

In spite of all the changes that occurred during this Europeanisation period, the performance of capitalism in the SE countries was still weak at the peak of the economic growth cycle (Sapir 2006; Hemerijck 2013, chapter 7). It was weaker than in the best European country performers but with clear differences between the four countries in both the dimensions of welfare capitalism performance: in efficiency, in terms of the level of labour market participation, and in equity, in terms of the capacity to reduce poverty risks (Figure 1). The performance was more positive in efficiency than in equity: in 2007 the employment rate of these countries was close to that of the EU-17, much closer than the percentage of the reduction of the poverty rate before and after social transfers. At that time Portugal exceeded the employment rate of the EU-17 and Spain equalled it; Greece shortened the distance to slightly less than four points and Italy remained the lowest performer at a distance of seven points. The four countries continued to have a significantly lower performance than the EU-17 in the capacity of poverty reduction. Portugal was slightly closer, reducing the poverty rate by a quarter. The other three countries reduced poverty much less, with Greece as the weakest country in this dimension.

The situation in these two dimensions has changed substantially since the Great Recession. Now the performance in the employment rate has placed the four countries well below the average level of the eurozone, although in very unequal relative positions. In the other dimension, however, the differences between the Southern countries continue to be important but three of these countries have improved their

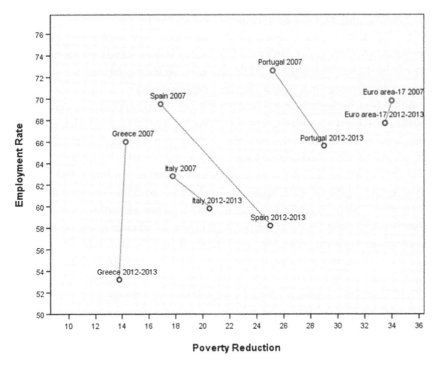

**Figure 1** Profiles of Southern European Countries on Employment Rate and Percentage of Poverty Rate Reduction before and after Social Transfers, 2007 and 2013
*Source*: EUROSTAT, EU-Labour Force Survey (EU-LFS) and EU-Statistics on Income and Living Conditions (EU-SILC).

relative efficiency in the reduction of poverty, especially Spain, while Greece sustains a similar level in this dimension.

### The Employment Crisis

As mentioned before, the trait of a low level of labour market participation attributed to these countries was not totally the case at the end of the growth cycle before the Great Recession (Figures 1 and 2). The employment achievements were very different in the four: Portugal had faced a slight increase during that growth phase, but still maintained high employment levels, well above those of the Eurozone (EU-17). Spain had increased its employment rate by almost 18 points since 1995 and had shortened its historical distance with reference to the EU-17. Italy and Greece had also substantially improved their employment levels, although they were not able to shorten the distances from the EU-17, nor the differences between them, which were favourable for Greece until very recently.

The Great Recession has caused an uneven employment crisis in each of these countries. Greece and Portugal have not only lost all employment improvements accumulated during the growth cycle, but they have also clearly worsened in terms of

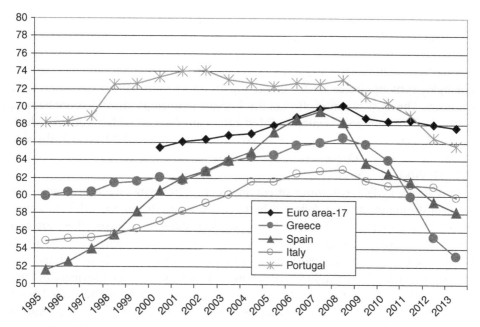

**Figure 2** Employment Rates 1995–2013 (20 to 64 years)
*Source*: EUROSTAT, EU-LFS.

employment level in comparison with the situation in 1995. Spain has lost 11.3 points in terms of employment rate, although it still maintains seven points of the total gained during the growth cycle. Italy has lost only 3.2 employment points during the crisis, but its employment level is still low due to the scarce improvement achieved during the previous cycle. The four countries remain far below the average employment levels of the eurozone, although distances are not even. Due to these facts, they remain very uneven in terms of unemployment although their relative positions have changed slightly.

Such huge employment losses will have consequences in the long run. It is very unlikely that these four countries will be able to achieve the Europe 2020 objectives (European Commission 2013b). Starting from the 2012 scenario, Greece and Spain would have a 14.7 point gap to reach the employment rates established as national targets by Europe 2020, the widest gap among all EU-27 countries. To reach the target both countries would have to increase those rates at an annual average growth of 2.9 points. Italy and Portugal would have narrower gaps, 7.0 and 8.5 points, respectively, but they are also among the highest in the EU-27 – only surpassed by Bulgaria and Hungary – and would also demand high annual average growth rates, of 1.5 and 1.7 points, respectively.

Due to these employment losses, the four countries have reached two-digit unemployment rates, the three countries facing the deepest employment crisis (Greece, Spain and Portugal) having matched the EU-17 levels before the crisis. At the end of 2013, two countries had tripled their unemployment figures – Greece to 27.2 and Spain to 26.1 per cent – while Portugal (16.3 per cent) had doubled it and Italy (11.4 per cent) had sustained an increase of more than four points. The relative weight of long-term unemployment (at least 12 months) amounted to two-thirds of the total unemployment in Greece in 2013, and slightly more than half in the other three countries. The most common effect of this increase in unemployment has not been an increase of 'discouraged unemployed', but rather an effect of 'added worker',[1] which has made activity rates increase in all countries, at least until 2012, with the sole exception of Italy (Organisation for Economic Cooperation and Development [OECD] 2013, pp. 25–26).

This strong cyclical behaviour of employment, a 'honeymoon' effect of high job creation during expansions followed by huge job losses during the crisis, is a trait shared by the four countries though to somewhat different degrees. There are two other traits relating to the groups most affected by the crisis of employment, which will be described below: the high volatility of youth employment, mostly temporary, and the vicious circle of low productivity, involving much more the employment of low-skilled workers. These three traits of performance are linked with two-tier labour market institutions, a trend that was not substantially modified in the cycles of reforms prior to the crisis (Boeri 2011), in a very unique way in Spain (Bentolila, Dolado & Jimeno 2012).

The Great Recession has not only reduced the employment level in these countries but also changed its composition in a substantial way. A singular trait of this employment crisis is the fact that it has affected all age, gender, education and wage groups, although quite unevenly in terms of intensity. This could have altered the more traditional patterns of employment participation in SE, namely, the typical predominance of male employment to the detriment of female employment, particularly in the central part of the life cycle, typical of the 'male breadwinner' model.

In terms of age and gender, to better show this important shift caused by the crisis, employment rates of three five-year age groups are considered. They are representative of three phases of the whole span of working life for each gender (Table 1). These employment rates clearly show the persistence of the said traditional pattern during

**Table 1** Employment Rates by Age and Sex, 2007 and 2013 (per cent)

|          | 25–29 years | | | | 40–44 years | | | | 55–59 years | | | |
|          | Males | | Females | | Males | | Females | | Males | | Females | |
|          | 2007 | 2013 | 2007 | 2013 | 2007 | 2013 | 2007 | 2013 | 2007 | 2013 | 2007 | 2013 |
|----------|------|------|------|------|------|------|------|------|------|------|------|------|
| EU-17    | 81.1 | 72.0 | 68.7 | 64.9 | 90.2 | 84.9 | 72.9 | 72.2 | 67.3 | 72.2 | 47.6 | 62.7 |
| Greece   | 81.3 | 53.2 | 62.6 | 43.4 | 93.3 | 78.9 | 65.1 | 55.3 | 73.5 | 59.7 | 33.6 | 53.6 |
| Spain    | 83.7 | 57.8 | 72.0 | 56.5 | 89.4 | 73.6 | 65.7 | 62.2 | 72.8 | 67.0 | 38.1 | 56.2 |
| Italy    | 73.4 | 59.7 | 55.1 | 45.8 | 91.3 | 84.2 | 61.5 | 60.5 | 59.0 | 70.4 | 33.8 | 55.3 |
| Portugal | 82.1 | 69.2 | 72.3 | 66.7 | 89.9 | 78.2 | 77.6 | 75.7 | 66.6 | 64.4 | 52.5 | 62.5 |

*Source*: EUROSTAT, EU-LFS.

the growth phase, above all during the mid and final stages of the working life. Before the crisis, the four countries showed situations close to full employment among prime-age male workers (40–44 years), substantially higher than the employment of women at that age. Employment rates of both genders were even more distant in the pre-retirement age group (50–59 years). However, the trait of low labour market participation by the young was not very characteristic of these countries. Spain and Portugal could reach the end of their growth cycle with very high youth employment rates (25–29 years) in comparative terms, as in 2007 they were above those of the EU-17 for both male and female jobs.

The employment crisis has been much harsher for the groups facing job insertion (25–29 years), even more so in the case of males than females, and especially for young males from Greece and Spain, who have lost around 25 points in their employment rates. As a result of the lower impact of the employment crisis on young women, in 2012 employment rates of males and females were already similar in Spain and Portugal, closer to Italian rates, and still far from those in Greece.

The fall of employment has also been important in the core ages of working life (40–44 years), and especially among males in Spain, Greece and Portugal with a loss of 15, 12 and 9 points, respectively in terms of employment rates. Therefore, in these three countries, the crisis has seriously harmed the labour positions of the traditional breadwinners of the Mediterranean model. In Greece and Spain, women in this age group also faced job losses, and therefore, the weakening of the position of the male breadwinner households could not be mitigated by the female employment rate in this age group.

Even older males, close to retirement age (55–59 years), have lost a great amount of employment, except for Italian males, who have improved the extremely low employment rate they had before the crisis. It has been very different for older women. They have maintained their employment levels in Greece and Portugal, very low comparatively in the former and quite high in the latter, whereas Spain and Italy have significantly improved previously low labour participation for this group despite the crisis.

Even though the crisis is showing a considerable youth bias, the intensity of this effect has been very uneven depending on the level of education. To analyse this, three groups of young people are examined, one for each education level, and in each case in an appropriate age group to allow sufficient labour integration time to have elapsed since leaving the education system. The age groups were 20–24 years for those who have just finished compulsory education (Isced97 0–2); 25–29 for those who completed the post-compulsory secondary level (Isced97 3–4); and 30–35 for those who experienced tertiary education (Isced97 5–6). These data clearly stress the huge negative impact of the crisis on the employment of young people with the lowest level of qualifications in the four countries. Among those aged 20–24 who have just finished compulsory education, in 2012 only approximately one in three were employed in Greece, Spain and Italy, and one in two in Portugal. In Spain this group saw its employment rate reduced by almost half with respect to the 2005 rate. But the young people with post-compulsory secondary level have also lost participation (except for Portugal), and to a lesser extent the young people with higher education, who in 2012 maintained employment rates of above 70 per cent in the 30–34 age group, in all the countries (Figure 3).

The non-occupation of non-qualified youths is not a problem caused by the crisis. During the economic boom, none of these countries managed to employ more than two-thirds of these young people; in Italy only half of them were employed. In the case of Spain, where this group was the most affected by the recession, each crisis since the 1980s gradually aggravated the uneven impact on the employment rates of the unqualified and qualified groups. The former group is the hardest hit by each crisis, and every subsequent growth period allows a smaller number of them to regain employment than the number who lost employment (Garrido & Gutiérrez 2011). This gradual 'chronification' of unemployment of the unqualified may be the most common problem shared by the labour markets in the four countries, a problem aggravated by the last recession but not caused by it.

Regarding employment composition by wage levels, during the growth period the main trends were upgrading. Against expectations that in the traditional SE the labour markets in these countries would tend either towards polarisation or downgrading, none of these four countries was characterised by these trends during the 1995–2006 period (Fernández-Macias, Hurley & Eurofound 2008). Greece modified its employment structure towards growth in the middle profile, with greater increases in medium-paid jobs. Italy and Spain underwent changes that increased the weight of medium and highly paid jobs, being therefore characterised as hybrid upgrading/ growth in the middle. Portugal faced a clearer upgrading transformation.

However, the evidence available for the crisis period shows predominant trends towards polarisation. At least during the first phase of the crisis (2008–10), this trend is very clear in the case of Spain, with relative employment losses that are highly

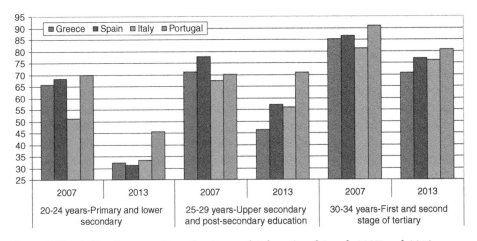

**Figure 3** Youth Employment Rates by Age and Educational Level, 2007 and 2013
*Source*: EUROSTAT, EU-LFS.

concentrated in medium-paid jobs, in the third and fourth quintile, and in Portugal with higher employment losses in the third quintile. In Greece and Italy, the changes present a different profile; in both cases there is a downgrading trend, much more obvious in the case of Italy, as the greatest employment losses occur in the highest area of the salary distribution, in the second quintile in Greece and in the first quintile in Italy. During the second and deepest phase of the crisis, and still based on sparse data, these trends are confirmed (European Commission 2013b). Spain, Greece and Portugal evolved towards a clearer polarisation in terms of employment, although with a slight upgrading tendency, losing employment above all in the central quintile, but also reducing employment at the ends, although more in the fourth and fifth quintiles than in the first and second. Italy reinforced its downgrading trend even more, increasing its employment in the two lower quintiles and decreasing it in the three higher quintiles, above all in the second.

In short, at the end of the growth cycle, these countries had been able to mitigate (Italy to a lesser extent) the most typical problem of their welfare capitalism model: the low employment level of youth and women, even notably improving the employment of women in the middle age group, whilst at the same time the traditional pattern of high employment of men was preserved. The Great Recession has had three effects very much shared by SE countries: firstly, the deep anti-youth bias of the employment crisis has done away with one of those two historical achievements; secondly, as adult male employment was so hard hit, it has weakened one of its most characteristic traits, namely, the male breadwinner; and, finally, the problem of unqualified unemployment has been aggravated, a problem that could be the most persistent and common trait in SE.

However, other aspects of employment composition by age and gender have shown different changes in each country. In Greece, which already had with low employment rates, the losses have affected all age groups in both genders. In Spain, the job losses have only exempted older women, who have even faced an improvement. In Portugal, the crisis has had a clear male bias, as the female employment level has hardly varied in the three age groups. In Italy, the crisis has aggravated the anti-youth bias that was already typical in this country, only weakly hitting male employment in the middle age groups, with some employment improvements for both older males and females.

These countries show more important differences in terms of unemployment protection, a factor with obvious potential consequences in poverty risk and income inequality. Reforms have been much softer than those in the employment protection field, probably because the severity of the crisis itself does not recommend decreases in such protection mechanisms. Only Portugal has introduced important reforms to reduce unemployment benefit and its duration. To broaden the protection, Greece, Spain and Portugal have introduced means-tested unemployment assistance or have increased the populations covered by this assistance, for situations of need once the unemployment benefits had been used up.

But the starting situations were different in each country. Spain and Portugal share a similar unemployment protection system with moderate coverage levels, with respect to both unemployment and other social assistance benefits: between 40 and 50 per cent of short- and long-term unemployment (STU and LTU) and 25 per cent if it is very long-term unemployment (VLTU). Greece also has a moderate level although with lower STU protection, an even lower LTU and a minimum level of VLTU. Italy is at the bottom compared with other European countries, with the lowest protection level for any of the unemployment modalities (European Commission 2013a, p. 93).

They differ even more in another aspect of unemployment protection: protection intensity, which is usually measured on the basis of net replacement rates (NRRs). This indicator shows the two variants of unemployment protection in these countries much more clearly (European Commission 2013a, p. 91). On the one hand are Spain and Portugal with average levels of salary replacement between 50 per cent (Spain) and 60 per cent (Portugal). Furthermore, these levels have not decreased during the crisis. On the other hand are Greece and Italy with much lower replacement levels that do not exceed 25 per cent in Greece or 10 per cent in Italy, where there has even been a slight decrease during the crisis.

## Poverty Risk

The available research on the relationship between the economic cycle and income inequality is not sufficiently conclusive. A strong decrease in employment usually affects households in the lower income distribution segment more than households in the middle and high segments. Both the comparative (Jenkins et al. 2012; Callan et al. 2011; Avram et al. 2012) and the national case studies (for Spain, Laparra & Pérez Eransus 2012; Fundación Alternativas 2013; for Greece, Matsaganis & Leventi 2013; and for Italy, Brandolini, D'Amuri & Faiella 2012) show that the impact in terms of poverty risk depends not only on the intensity of the employment crisis but on a variety of factors affecting income distribution. Moreover, the duration of the crisis may result in its severest effects only being felt in more recent years, with limited data currently available.[2]

These countries used to share high levels of income inequality, as shown by the two most common indicators, poverty risk and Gini coefficient (Figure 4). They also – except Portugal – shared a low capacity to reduce poverty (Figure 1). However, the recent evolution of these indicators differs by slight but relevant degrees. Spain and Greece have pursued pathways in which poverty and inequality follow opposite directions to those of the economic cycle. They have decreased, although very slightly, during growth and increased during the crisis. Italy and Portugal pursue pathways that are less parallel to the economic cycle: Portugal shows a decreasing trend in poverty and inequality from 2005 to 2010, although this shifted in 2011; Italy, on the other hand, shows a similar trend to that of Portugal in terms of Gini coefficient and more parallel to the economic cycle regarding poverty risk.

As in the case of the poverty indicator, the Gini coefficient illustrates that these countries have become slightly more similar in terms of income distribution. This is the result, above all, of the different evolution of this coefficient in Portugal and Spain,

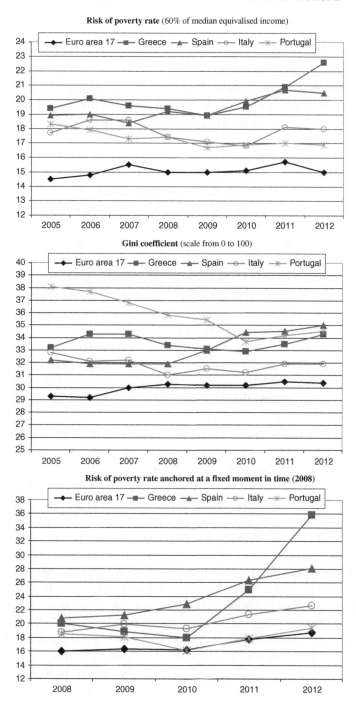

**Figure 4** Indicators of Income Inequality in SE Countries, 2005–12
*Source*: EUROSTAT, EU-SILC.

which were the countries with, respectively, the highest and lowest levels of income inequality. In Spain, inequality has increased since 2009 and in Portugal it decreased until 2010 followed by a slight rise in the two most recent years.

The poverty risk with a fixed threshold at the beginning of the crisis provide another useful reference, as it allows us to identify the potential change of poverty risk if the whole income distribution had not changed. It confirms the current increases in the poverty risk in the four countries if the threshold were maintained at the beginning of the crisis (2008). This increase is comparatively higher in Greece, where the poverty risk rate would double, and where somewhat more than two out of three people would be poor in 2012 with the 2008 threshold. In the other countries, the poverty risk increases are continuous but much less intense, in such a way that this indicator only increases by 4–6 points with reference to that based on a mobile threshold. This fact shows that in Greece the income decrease in households in the lowest part of the distribution is far higher than that in the other three countries.

It could be stated that the crisis phase has made the four countries much more similar than they used to be in terms of their capacity to protect from the poverty risk by most frequent activity status (Figure 5). Before the crisis, differences in that feature between Italy and the other three countries were much more important than now. Italy showed, and still shows, a pattern of greater capacity to protect people from the poverty risk, especially the retired and also the employed, as opposed to a much lower capacity to avoid that risk among the unemployed. The other three countries were very similar regarding their respective poverty risks for each of those groups: low among the unemployed and high among the employed and retired. During the crisis, this pattern has not undergone significant modification, but some trends have been identified wherein the poverty risk rates of the three groups have narrowed. The most prominent trends in this direction have been the poverty risk increase of the unemployed in the four countries, at a faster pace in the three countries where it was lower (Greece, Spain and Portugal), as well as the decrease in the poverty risk of the retired, also in all the countries, but especially apposite in Spain.

However, when the poverty risk is measured on the basis of the indicators addressing its most concerning aspects, persistence and material privation, the relative scenario of these countries is very different. Only households with children are examined, to focus on situations in which these poverty risks would have potentially more negative consequences due to the presence of dependent minors (Figure 6). In Spain, regardless of the employment crisis intensity and the relevant deterioration of low incomes, the low levels of persistent poverty and severe material privation have hardly worsened. In Greece, however, persistent poverty increased constantly from 2007 until it affected one out of five households with children in 2011. During this time, there was also an important increase of severe material privation in this country. In Portugal, persistent poverty also rocketed in 2010 and 2011, although it was able to maintain its normally high level of material privation. In Italy, the trend to reduce the country's high persistent poverty was halted and severe material privation increased markedly from 2011 until it affected more than one out of ten households with children.

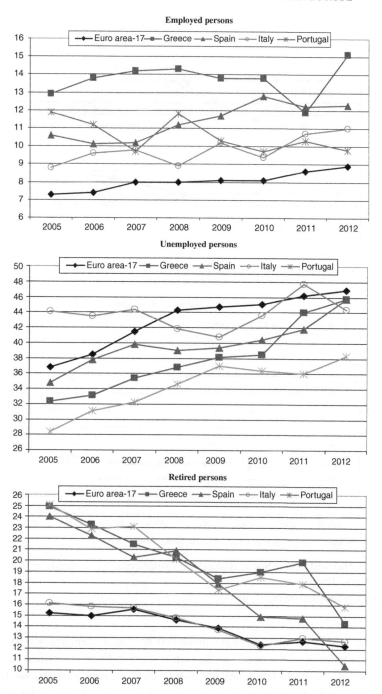

**Figure 5** Risk of Poverty Rates by Most Frequent Activity Status, 2005–12 (60 per cent of Median Equivalised Income)
*Source*: EUROSTAT, EU-SILC.

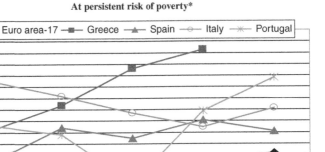

**At persistent risk of poverty***

*At-risk-of-poverty for the current year and at least two out of the preceding three years

**Severe material deprivation* rate**

*Inability to pay for at least four of nine deprivation items.

**Figure 6** Indicators of Severe Social Risks in SE Countries in Households with Dependent Children, 2005–12
*Source*: EUROSTAT, EU-SILC.

The weak poverty reduction effect produced by social transfers was one of the typical characteristics of the social protection system in these countries, particularly when pensions are excluded; namely, taking into account only social transfers, targeting potentially active population and households. This poverty risk protection effect is one of the basic functions of the social protection system. The risks prompted by employment crisis periods are one of the main proofs of its efficacy. In this sense, the crisis has shown that the ability to reduce the poverty risks by means of social transfers, starting from low comparative levels, became much more uneven in these countries, even more so in terms of the most severe poverty risk (Figure 7).

This reduction effect was very low in Greece and Italy and is still very similar during the crisis. It did not reach 20 per cent reduction, for a 60 per cent poverty threshold, and slightly surpassed 25 per cent of the most severe poverty (at a 40 per cent threshold). In 2012 the reduction rates of both poverty levels hardly varied in either country. However, Portugal and Spain, with a slight risk reduction before the crisis, faced a greater reduction in 2012, especially in the case of severe poverty risk (40 per cent threshold). This risk was reduced by slightly more than 40 per cent in Spain and 45 per cent in Portugal as a consequence of social transfers.

There are three factors that could explain the variety of national profiles in poverty risk during this period. The first factor is undoubtedly the composition of those affected by the employment crisis and how the potential income losses harm them and other groups. The second is how the specificities of the national system of social benefits and taxes interact with those profiles of income and employment losses. A third factor, the impact of austerity measures in those countries, can be taken into account although until now it has only been addressed by simulation approaches (Avram et al. 2012). Taking these factors into consideration, a synthetic picture of the specific profiles for each county can be provided.

Spain is the country with a greater increase in poverty risk, even more when measured with fixed thresholds. Nevertheless, Spain shows two traits that indicate smoother crisis impacts. On the one hand, the poverty risk of the unemployed is still comparatively low. On the other hand, persistent poverty and severe material privation were already low and have hardly deteriorated. The Spanish profile could be explained by the following factors. Firstly, the concentration of employment loss among the least qualified people has impacted on labour incomes at the end of

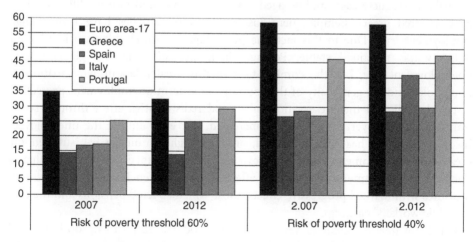

**Figure 7** Percentage Reduction of Poverty Rates before and after Social Transfers (pensions excluded), 2007 and 2012
*Source*: EUROSTAT, EU-SILC.

the distribution to a greater extent. Secondly, income loss in that area has not translated into major leaps of unemployment or persistent poverty, as in Greece or Italy. This is mainly due to two reasons: the high rotation of the Spanish labour market, which has reduced the weight of long-term unemployment, and the relative generosity of the unemployment protection for long-term unemployment. This aspect is consistent with another observed fact: the system of social transfers (excluding pensions) has maintained a moderate poverty reduction effect, even in the case of the deepest poverty risk (40 per cent threshold). The stability of this poverty risk reduction effect may be related to a third factor, the fiscal consolidation measures implemented during the crisis, for which the available simulations point towards a gradual joint effect in Spain, the richest groups contributing with greater relative reductions of income.

In the case of Greece, the employment crisis has enjoyed a similar intensity and profile to that in Spain, although in this country the employment loss has been higher in the middle-aged and older population, as well as the employed with middle and high education levels. Although poverty does not show large variations, the poverty risk of the unemployed, persistent poverty and material privation have become especially high. This more alarming poverty pattern (due to the poverty of the unemployed and poverty persistence) could be mainly linked to the very weak impact on poverty reduction of mid- and long-term unemployment schemes. Two further factors may explain the stability of inequality indicators. These are the loss of labour income in all the distribution segments and the joint effect of austerity measures, as in Greece taxes and public sector wage cuts have had a strong progressive impact, and the measures regarding pensions are also progressive, although their impact is lower. This progressive effect has only been compensated by the regressive impact of value added tax (VAT) and of social benefits (excluding pensions).

In the Portuguese case, middle-aged and young males and non-qualified workers have suffered great unemployment losses, but adult females have kept a high employment level. Due to this fact, the percentage of households with low labour intensity has remained stable. Portugal had, and still has, a high long-term unemployment rate, but the combination of this greater labour participation of households and the generosity of the country's long-term unemployment protection system has allowed the preservation of a good redistributive effect through social transfers. Thus, poverty risk has not increased, not even among the unemployed. Income inequality has even decreased, and the highest quintile has suffered the greatest relative income loss. To a great extent, this is also explained by the fact that in Portugal the adjustments that deeply affect all incomes enclosed two adjustment measures with marked progressive effects, those which affected pensions and the cuts in public workers' earnings.

Finally, in Italy the changes have been more moderate in terms of job losses and effects on inequality. Job losses have been concentrated among the young and, as the high employment levels among middle-aged and older adults have remained stable, the level and distribution of labour income have been maintained. The poverty and inequality levels have been very stable on almost all the indicators, except for the unemployed poverty rate, which has increased by one point, although it was already high before the crisis. The protective weakness of unemployment benefits explains that fact, and probably also the recent leap in severe material privation. Furthermore, the adjustment measures have had quite a flat effect: the changes in income taxes have had the deepest impact but they have also resulted in a very similar income loss in all areas of the scale. Changes in public sector pensions and salaries, with a more progressive impact, have compensated the flat effect on taxes, which per se would have harmed the households with lowest incomes even more, and subsequently would have increased the poverty risk.

## Conclusion

The Great Recession has provided a somewhat distorted image of the performance of the Mediterranean welfare states. The magnitude of the employment crisis and the growing inequality of incomes in these countries have reinforced the image of a very homogeneous and very weak welfare system, particularly in the main dimensions of performance, namely participation in employment and the ability to reduce the risk of poverty. This article has shown that this image is only partially true.

In the dimension of participation in employment, the similarities between these countries are still quite evident. Even with the unequal size of the crisis and some different nuances in their composition of age and sex, the countries still share two traits: on the one hand, the low and secondary occupation of the young; on the other, the unemployment, increasingly structural, of the less skilled. A third characteristic, the very cyclical behaviour of employment, is less common. It is not shared by Italy but is very marked in Greece and Spain, the countries where the employment crisis has been most intense.

It is noteworthy that those three features of the crisis of employment in these countries are linked to the dualism of their labour markets. The modernisation and recalibration of the welfare systems that these countries carried out during their Europeanisation failed to replace this pattern with another, more inclusive one, especially in Spain and Greece. The institutional reforms of the labour market carried out in response to the crisis, deeper in Italy and Spain, do not yet seem to constitute an exit strategy from dualism, although it is early to assess their impact.

On the other dimension of performance – poverty and the capacity to reduce it – there is less similarity among these countries. They have only shared one trait: the bias towards protecting the elderly, which is still very visible. Despite the reforms of the pension system in the previous stage and cuts during the crisis, all of them have significantly reduced poverty among the retired. However, other components of the system of protection, such as the protection of unemployment or minimum guarantees, have had very uneven development in the four countries and play a very important role when one compares income inequality and the capacity to reduce poverty. The improvement in the capacity to reduce poverty and maintain a moderate risk of material deprivation in Spain and Portugal, at least in the first stage of the crisis, must be attributed to these two devices.

Anyway, the minimum income system in these countries, even of the most generous, was not able effectively to confront poverty risk before the crisis, and much less during it. In addition, the risks of poverty – for which comparative data are still not available – may have increased in recent years due to the increase in long-term employment and the lower number of unemployed people with unemployment insurance, and public resources for minimum incomes are running out due to fiscal consolidation. The beginning of the way out of the crisis should encourage a scenario in which these countries will tackle reform of their system of guaranteeing minimums, along with reforms of their systems of protection for the long-term unemployed.

## Notes

1. The 'added worker' refers to an increase in the labour supply of married women when their husbands become unemployed.
2. The most recent EU-SILC provided by Eurostat are for 2012 and it should be noted that income data are for the previous year.

## References

Avram, S., Figari, F., Leventi, Ch., Levy, H., Navicke, J., Matsaganis, M., Militaru, E., Paulus, A., Rastrigina, O. & Sutherland, H. (2012) 'The distributional effects of fiscal consolidation in nine EU countries', Research note 01/2012 European Observatory on the Social Situation and Demography, European Commission.

Bentolila, S., Dolado, J. J. & Jimeno, J. F. (2012) 'Reforming an insider-outsider labor market: the Spanish experience', CES IFO Working Paper, no 3760.

Boeri, T. (2011) 'Institutional reforms and dualism in European labor markets', in *Handbook of Labor Economics*, eds D. Card, O. Ashenfelter & B. Part, Part B. 4th edn. Elsevier, Amsterdam, pp. 1173–1236.

Brandolini, A., D'Amuri, F. & Faiella, I. (2012) 'Country case study – Italy', in *The Great Recession and the Distribution of Household Income*, eds S. Jenkins, A. Brandolini, J. Micklewright & B. Nolan, Oxford University Press, Oxford.

Cabrero, G. (2011) 'The consolidation of the Spanish Welfare State (1972–2010)', in *The Spanish Welfare Sate in the European Context*, eds A. M. Guillén & M. León, Ashgate, Farnham, pp. 17–38.

Callan, T., Leventi, Ch., Levy, H., Matsaganis, M., Paulus, A. & Sutherland, H. (2011) 'The distributional effect of austerity measures: a comparison of six EU countries', EUROMOD Working Paper, no. EM6/11, available online at: https://www.iser.essex.ac.uk/euromod/working-papers

Capucha, L., Bomba, T., Fernández, R. & Matos, G. (2005) 'Portugal: a virtuous oOath towards minimun income?', in *Welfare State Reform in Southern Europe: Fighting Poverty and Social Inclusion in Italy, Spain, Portugal and Greece*, ed. M. Ferrera, Routledge, London, pp. 204–265.

European Commission (2013a) *Employment and Social Developments in Europe 2012*, Publications Office of the European Union, Luxembourg.

European Commission (2013b) *EU Employment and Social Situation-Quarterly Review, September 2013*, Publications Office of the European Union, Luxembourg.

Fernández-Macías, E., Hurley, J. & Eurofound (2008) *More and better jobs? Patterns of employment expansion in Europe ERM report 2008*, Publications Office of the European Union, Luxembourg.

Ferrera, M. (1996) 'The '"Southern Model"' of welfare in social Europe', *Journal of European Social Policy*, vol. 6, no. 1, pp. 17–37.

Ferrera, M. (ed.) (2005) *Welfare State Reform in Southern Europe. Fighting Poverty and Social Exclusion in Italy, Spain, Portugal and Greece*, Routledge, London.

Ferrera, M. (2010) 'The South European Countries', in *The Oxford Handbook of the Welfare State*, eds F. G. Castles, S. Leibfried, J. Lewis, H. Obinger & C. Pierson, Oxford University Press, Oxford, pp. 616–629.

Ferrera, M. & Gualmini, E. (2000) 'Reforms guided by consensus: the welfare state in the Italian transition', *West European Politics*, vol. 23, no. 2, pp. 187–208.

Ferrera, M. & Hemerijck, A. (2003) 'Recalibrating European welfare regimes', in *Governing Work and Welfare in a New Economy: European and American Experiments*, eds J. Zeitlin & D. Trubeck, Oxford University Press, Oxford, pp. 88–128.

Fundación Alternativas (2013) *Primer Informe sobre la Desigualdad en España 2013*, Fundación Alternativas, Madrid.

Garrido, L. & Gutiérrez, R. (2011) 'La reforma ineludible. Regularidades e inercias del mercado de trabajo en España', *Panorama Social*, vol. 13, pp. 37–54.

Guillén, A. M. (2010) 'Defrosting the Spanish Welfare state: the weight of conservative components', in *A Long Goodbye to Bismarck?* ed. B. Palier, Amsterdam University Press, Amsterdam, pp. 183–206.

Guillén, A. M. & Matsaganis, M. (2000) 'Testing the 'Social Dumping' hypothesis in Southern Europe', *Journal of European Social Policy*, vol. 10, no. 2, pp. 120–145.

Guillén, A., Álvarez, S. & Adao e Silva, P. (2003) 'Redesigning the Spanish and Portuguese welfare states: the Impact of accession into the European Union', *South European Society and Politics*, vol. 8, no. 1-2, pp. 231–268.

Guillén, A. M. & León, M. (2011) *The Spanish Welfare State in European Context*, Ahsgate, Farnham.

Hemejrick, A. (2013) *Changing Welfare States*, Oxford University Press, Oxford.

Jenkins, S., Brandolini, A., Micklewright, J. & Nolan, B. (eds) (2012) *The Great Recession and the Distribution of Household Income*, Oxford University Press, Oxford.

Jesuola, M. & Alti, T. (2010) 'Italy: An Incomplete Departure From Bismarck', in *A Long Goodbye to Bismarck?* ed. B. Palier, Amsterdam University Press, Amsterdam, pp. 157–182.

Karamessini, M. (2008) 'Continuity and change in the Southern European social model', *International Labour Review*, vol. 147, no. 1, pp. 43–70.

Laparra, M. & Pérez-Eransus, B.(cords) (2012) *Crisis y fractura social en Europa. Causas y efectos en España*, Obra Social La Caixa, Barcelona.

Marí-Klose, P. & Moreno-Fuentes, F. J. (2013) 'The Southern European welfare model in the post-industrial order', *European Societies*, vol. 15, no. 4, pp. 475–492.

Mato, J. (2011) 'Spain: fragmented unemployment protection in a segmented labour market', in *Regulating the Risk of Unemployment*, eds J. Clasen & D. Clegg, Oxford University Press, Oxford, pp. 146–186.

Matsaganis, M. (2005) 'Greece: fighting with hands tied behind the back', in *Welfare State Reform in Southern Europe: Fighting Poverty and Social Inclusion in Italy, Spain, Portugal and Greece*, ed. M. Ferrera, Routledge, London, pp. 33–83.

Matsaganis, M. & Leventi, C. (2013) 'The distributional impact of the Greek crisis in 2010', *Fiscal Studies*, vol. 34, no. 1, pp. 83–108.

OECD. (2013) *Employment Outlook 2013*, available online: ww.oecd.org/about/publishing/Corrigendum_oecd-employment-outlook-2013.pdf.

Petmesidou, M. & Papatheodorou, C. (eds) (2006) *Poverty and Social Deprivation in the Mediterranean: Trends, Policies and Welfare Prospects in the New Millenium*, Zed Books, London.

Sachi, S. & Bastagli, F. (2005) 'Italy: striving uphill but stopping halfway', in *Welfare State Reform in Southern Europe. Fighting Poverty and Social Exclusion in Italy, Spain, Portugal and Greece*, ed. M Ferrera, Routledge, London, pp. 84–140.

Sapir, A. (2006) 'Globalization and the reform of European social models', *Journal of Common Market Studies*, vol. 44, no. 2, pp. 369–390.

Spanou, C. & Sotiropoulos, D. A. (2011) 'The odyssey of administrative reforms in Greece, 1981-2009: a tale of two reform paths', *Public Administration*, vol. 89, no. 3, pp. 723–737.

# The Distributional Impact of Austerity and the Recession in Southern Europe

Manos Matsaganis and Chrysa Leventi

*Southern European welfare states are under stress. On the one hand, the recession has been causing unemployment to rise and incomes to fall. On the other hand, austerity has affected the capacity of welfare states to protect those affected. This paper assesses the distributional implications of the crisis in Greece, Spain, Italy and Portugal from 2009 to 2013. Using a microsimulation model, we disentangle the first-order effects of tax–benefit policies from the broader effects of the crisis, and estimate how its burden has been shared across income groups. We conclude by discussing the methodological pitfalls and policy implications of our research.*

In recent years the world economy has been in turmoil. The global financial crisis of 2007–09 was followed by the sovereign debt crisis of 2011–13, interrupted by a modest recovery. Several authors have labelled this the 'Great Recession' (Jenkins et al. 2013), as it is affecting large areas of the globe, and because its duration and depth exceed those of previous downturns. In Europe, the combined gross domestic product (GDP) of the 27 European Union (EU) member states contracted by 4.5 per cent in 2009 relative to the year before. It subsequently recovered somewhat, but once again registered negative growth in 2012 and stagnated in 2013. Overall, by 2013 the European economy had shrunk by 1.2 per cent relative to its 2008 level.

The recession was an archetypal asymmetric shock, as some countries were affected much more than others. In Greece the size of the economy declined by over 23 per cent in 2007–13. In Portugal and Spain, the size of the contraction from peak (2008) to trough (2013) was around seven per cent, in Italy almost nine per cent (in 2007–13). Unemployment in the EU rose by 3.6 percentage points (ppts) in 2007–13 (Eurostat 2014). Again, things were much worse in those countries worst hit by the crisis, and especially in Greece and Spain, where the unemployment rate went up by as many as 19 and 18 ppts, respectively (in 2007–13).

Spending on social protection in the EU (as percentage of GDP) peaked in 2009, levelled out in 2010 and decreased in 2011 (Eurostat 2014). Based on national accounts data, Bontout and Lokajickova (2013) found that the downward trend in social expenditure accelerated in 2012. The fall in social spending since 2011 can be partly attributed to the recovery and subsequent employment growth, as experienced in some parts of the EU. However, reductions in social expenditure were also significant in countries that were still deep in recession, such as Greece and Portugal. This is in sharp contrast to the notion that, in a crisis, social benefits can act as 'social stabilisers' (Dolls, Fuest & Peichl 2012; Salgado et al. 2014).

As a matter of fact, cuts in social protection were often a component of austerity policies. In response to the crisis, bailout deals were offered to Ireland, Greece, Cyprus, Latvia, Hungary, Portugal and Romania. These were made conditional upon satisfactory progress on a detailed set of fiscal cuts and policy reforms. The pressure resulting from external constraints was also unmistakeable in Spain and Italy, even though softer forms of conditionality prevailed there.

The aim of this paper is to provide an early assessment of the distributional implications of the Great Recession in 2009–13 in four southern European countries severely affected by it: Greece, Spain, Italy and Portugal. Using a microsimulation model, we attempt to quantify the impact of tax–benefit policies (such as fiscal consolidation measures) and of some of the most important developments in the wider economy (namely changes in individuals' labour market status and market incomes) on income distribution. Moreover, we estimate how the burden of the crisis (taken from now on to signify the combined effect of tax–benefit policies and broader economic developments) has been shared across income groups, and how the differential impact of the crisis may have altered the composition of the population in poverty.

The paper is structured as follows. We first provide a review of the literature on the interactions of fiscal consolidation with inequality and growth, including key findings of microsimulation studies. We continue by explaining the methodology of our work. We then present our estimates of the distributional effects of the Great Recession in Greece, Spain, Italy and Portugal. We conclude by summarising the most important findings, and by reflecting on the policy implications of this research.


## Literature Review

### Interactions of Austerity with Growth

There can be little doubt that fiscal consolidation interacts with growth. On the one hand, austerity policies cause aggregate demand to fall and therefore lead firms catering for the domestic market to reduce output, cut salaries and lay off personnel. On the other hand, the recession will weaken the deficit-reducing potential of austerity policies and may lead to calls for the adoption of harsher measures.

This raises the question of how austerity contributes to the intensity of the recession. This is at the heart of the controversy on 'fiscal multipliers', i.e. the output loss associated with fiscal consolidation. The issue gained increasing importance in the wake of the current crisis and initiated a heated debate. On the whole, international organisations such as the International Monetary Fund (IMF) (2012) and the Organisation for Economic Cooperation and Development (OECD) (2014) now accept that they have underestimated the size of fiscal multipliers and have overestimated growth prospects. In contrast, the European Commission (EC) has suggested that forecast errors may be due to the negative response of investors towards heavily indebted countries rather than an underestimation of the fiscal multiplier (EC 2012), while the European Central Bank (ECB) has argued that the medium- and long-term effects of fiscal consolidation more than compensate for any short-term output losses (ECB 2012).

In general, the relationship between changes in government expenditure and growth is non-linear (Barro 1990). The actual effect will depend on a variety of factors. To start with, fiscal multipliers tend to be larger when the economy is in recession than when it is in expansion (Auerbach & Gorodnichenko 2012; Corsetti, Meier & Müller 2012; Eyraud & Weber 2013). Also, output losses will be greater when efforts to improve fiscal balances take place simultaneously across several countries (Goujard 2013).

On the other hand, the policy mix of fiscal consolidation packages may also matter, although the evidence here is mixed. Some authors (Romer & Romer 2010; Alesina & Ardagna 2012; Alesina, Favero & Giavazzi 2012) have argued that declines in public spending may lead to stronger economic growth than is the case with tax increases, while others (Jordà & Taylor 2013; Ball et al. 2013) have found that the medium-term relationship of spending cuts with GDP growth is negative. Finally, the size of the multiplier will also depend on the characteristics of the economy under consideration. As argued by Alcidi and Gros (2012), output losses following fiscal consolidation will be inversely related to the savings rate, the average tax rate and the degree of trade openness.

### Interactions of Austerity with Inequality

While fiscal consolidation policies are widely held to cause poverty and inequality to rise, establishing their distributional effects is less straightforward than appears at first sight. Empirical evidence has shown that austerity does not necessarily have to be regressive. A study of fiscal consolidation in 18 countries in 1970–2010 by Agnello and Sousa (2012) found that fiscal adjustment programmes that took care to minimise adverse distributional effects had a higher probability of being successful. However, an analysis of 173 episodes of fiscal consolidation in 17 countries over the past 30 years by Ball, Leigh and Loungani (2011) showed that, on balance, adjustment costs were not shared equally, with lower-income groups experiencing heavier losses, and wages declining more than profits.

The size and make-up of fiscal consolidation may be crucial in determining the distributional impact of the adjustment. Agnello and Sousa (2012), mentioned above, found that the decline in income inequality following episodes of fiscal consolidation tended to take place where the policy mix relied more heavily on tax increases than on spending cuts. Woo et al. (2013) came to the same conclusion after analysing consolidation programmes in 17 countries in 1978–2009. Ahren, Arnold and Moeser (2011) found that progressive taxation and generous unemployment benefits can smooth the distributional impact of a financial crisis and fiscal consolidation.

In other words, an insidious trade-off could be at work. Progressive policies (such as raising personal income taxes) may reduce inequality at the cost of damaging long-term growth, while regressive policies (such as raising indirect taxes) may have the opposite effect (OECD 2013). In view of this, the static effects of austerity policies may be at odds with their dynamic effects.

*Estimating Distributional Effects via Microsimulation*

Microsimulation has been extensively used as a tool for assessing the distributional impact of the recent economic downturn and examining the effects of various austerity measures on income distribution.

In a single-country setting – Ireland – Callan, Nolan and Walsh (2011) assessed the impact of public sector pay cuts in 2009–10. These were found to be progressive against a counterfactual scenario of a four per cent cut in both public and private sector pay. Nolan, Callan and Maître (2013) expanded that analysis to include the overall distributional impact of tax and welfare changes over the period 2009–11, and again found the result to be highly progressive. In Italy, Brandolini, D'Amuri and Faiella (2013) replicated employment dynamics in 2007–10 and estimated the resulting variations in income flows. In the light of their findings they argued that the impact of the recent recession on inequality and poverty in the country has been fairly limited, despite the considerable fall in average income. In Greece, Leventi and Matsaganis (2013) estimated how the burden of the crisis was shared across the population in 2009–12. Their findings suggest that the rise in inequality began a year after the onset of the crisis, and gathered speed as the recession deepened. In Cyprus, Koutsampelas and Polycarpou (2013) assessed the distributional effects of the austerity measures introduced in 2011–12. Their analysis showed that most of the first-order effects of adjustment fell upon households located in the middle and upper part of the income distribution. In the UK, the effects of recent tax–benefit reforms were analysed by Browne and Levell (2010), Brewer, Browne and Joyce (2011) and Joyce and Sibieta (2013). Their findings suggest that those with the lowest incomes were the biggest losers from these policy changes.

In a comparative setting, Avram et al. (2013) simulated the distributional effects of fiscal consolidation measures up to 2012 in nine EU countries. The study showed that the burden of austerity was shared in very different ways in the countries considered. Finally, Bargain et al. (2013) examined the distributional impact of the economic crisis in France, Germany, the UK and Ireland in the period 2008–10 and the contribution of tax–benefit policy changes. They found that in all countries but Germany policy reactions contributed to stabilising or even reducing inequality and relative poverty.

## Methodology

### Departures from Previous Research

In assessing the distributional impact of tax–benefit policies, most of the time the choice of the underlying (market) income distribution may not matter much. However, at times of major changes, the assessment of the progressivity or otherwise of policies may differ significantly according to whether these are assessed on the distribution of market incomes at the beginning or at the end of the period under consideration. In Avram et al. (2013) the distributional effects of policy changes from 2009 to 2012 were evaluated on the assumption that 2009 policies were implemented on the 2012 market income distribution. In this paper we model the distributional effects of policies in the period 2009–13 on a year-by-year basis, rather than cumulatively. Policy changes between two consecutive years, say $t - 1$ and $t$, are assessed on the income distribution of year $t - 1$.

Also, as the literature reviewed above suggests, tax–benefit policies clearly affect market incomes. Ignoring these dynamic (indirect) policy effects leaves out an important part of the picture. Our approach departs from most of the studies reviewed above, where broader economic developments are explicitly excluded from the scope of the analysis. Rather than abstracting from them, this research attempts to locate first-order policy effects within the broader distributional effects of the crisis, by taking into account two important aspects of the latter: changes in market incomes and labour market transitions. By doing so, it also differs from Brandolini, D'Amuri and Faiella (2013), who assume wages, self-employment earnings and pension entitlements to have remained unchanged during the period under examination.

### Model and Data

We rely on the European tax–benefit model EUROMOD. The model uses survey data on gross incomes, labour market status and other characteristics of individuals and households, which it then applies to the tax–benefit rules in place in order to simulate direct taxes, social insurance contributions and entitlements to cash benefits. The components of the tax–benefit system that cannot be simulated (for example, those depending on prior contributions) are read off the data. The underlying micro data for all countries are drawn from the 2010 European Union Statistics on Income and Living Conditions (EU-SILC), reporting incomes earned in 2009. EUROMOD has been validated at both micro and macro level and has been tested in several applications. For a comprehensive overview, see Sutherland and Figari (2013).

The most important advantages of microsimulation in general, and EUROMOD in particular, are twofold: timeliness and attribution. Due to the complexity of income surveys, relevant income data only become available after considerable (i.e. 2–3 years') delay. In the meantime, EUROMOD can bridge the gap, by providing an early evaluation of changes in the income distribution of EU countries up to 2013. It can be used to disentangle the effects of each policy or other macroeconomic developments, taking into account the complex ways in which taxes interact with benefits and with each other. A direct analysis of actual data, when these become available, cannot do this as well.

*Accounting for Labour Market Developments*

A standard practice in static microsimulation models is to assume that the labour market characteristics of the population remain unchanged. Although this is a plausible assumption in a stable macro-economic environment, it may bias the results in periods of economic turbulence. Given the magnitude of changes in the countries under examination, disregarding such a development would have been inappropriate for the purposes of this research. Linking economy-wide changes to micro-level analysis is not a new idea. Elaborate simulation methodologies and techniques have been developed by the World Bank and have been used in several applications (see Bourguignon, Bussolo & Da Silva 2008).

In this paper changes in labour market status were taken into account following the approach adopted by Leventi et al. (2013). This approach can be briefly summarised as follows. Observations are selected on the basis of conditional probabilities of being employed. A logit model is used to estimate probabilities for working age individuals in the EUROMOD input data. The model is estimated separately for individuals with higher and lower levels of education. The weighted total number of observations that are selected to go through transitions based on their probabilities corresponds to the relative net change in employment levels by age group, gender and education as shown in the Labour Force Survey (LFS) statistics. Changes from short-term to long-term unemployment are also modelled based on a similar selection procedure as the one described above.

Labour market characteristics and sources of income are adjusted for those observations that are subject to transitions. In particular, employment/self-employment income is set to zero for individuals who become unemployed. For individuals moving from unemployment into employment, earnings are set equal to the mean among those already employed within the same stratum.

It should be noted that initial (i.e. 2009) employment rates do not align perfectly between EU-SILC and the LFS. Differences are mainly due to discrepancies in the structure of the underlying working age populations and the different way labour market status is measured. Hence, the aim of this adjustment is not to match the EUROMOD and LFS employment patterns in absolute terms but to account for relative changes in employment levels. Moreover, although focusing on net changes in employment rates allows EUROMOD to capture the employment dynamics shown by LFS, it does not fully capture compositional changes in the population of employed and unemployed which may have taken place within the period of analysis.

Finally, whereas changes in the labour market were carefully taken into account, no similar adjustments were made to account for demographic changes or changes in characteristics of the population such as education level or household structure. Arguably, these adjustments are less critical within the time frame studied, as major shifts are unlikely to happen in such a short period.

*Updating Market Incomes and Simulating Policies*

The non-availability, at the time of writing, of 'real' data for the time period in question implied that a synthetic income distribution had to be created for these years. As is standard practice in microsimulation, this involved two additional steps: updating incomes from the EU-SILC income reference period (2009) to the latest policy year (2013) and simulating tax−benefit policies.

Updating incomes is performed using factors based on the available administrative or survey statistics. Specific updating factors are derived for each income source, reflecting the change in their average amount between the income data reference period and the target year. Accurately capturing the evolution of employment income is of utmost importance for studying changes in the disposable income of households. In order to account for differential growth rates in employment income, updating factors are disaggregated by economic sector and by private and public sector in countries where such information is available.

Since EU-SILC provides no information on consumption, changes in indirect taxation are beyond the scope of this analysis. Changes in the provision of benefits in kind (such as health care, education, child care, etc.) are also not considered in this study. Simulations are carried out on the basis of the tax−benefit rules in place on 30 June of each policy year. In order to enhance the credibility of estimates, an effort has been made to address issues such as tax evasion (e.g. in Greece and Italy) and benefit non-take-up (e.g. in Greece). However, such adjustments are not possible to implement in all countries due to data limitations.

The full list of factors used for the uprating of original incomes and non-simulated benefits as well as detailed description of the way in which tax−benefit policies are simulated can be found in the EUROMOD Country Reports (EUROMOD 2014).

*Modelling the Distributional Effects of Austerity and the Crisis*

Drawing on the decomposition approach developed by Bargain and Callan (2010), we can approximate the *first-order* distributional effects of policies by simulating a hypothetical counterfactual scenario, capturing the effect of changes in policies on the income distribution as observed before these policies are actually implemented (i.e. typically at the time policy changes are announced and/or legislated). Since this is the only distribution known to policymakers when they take decisions on policy changes, we believe that estimating this hypothetical scenario is of interest and relevance.

More formally, household disposable income in our counterfactual scenario is constructed on the basis of:

(i) individuals' labour market status in year $t - 1$;
(ii) market incomes (other than public sector pay) in year $t - 1$;
(iii) tax and benefit polices in year $t$.

This is compared with the situation where all variables are set as in year t − 1. Note that in this counterfactual scenario we do not allow monetary parameters of taxes and benefits to grow from one year to another (by using for example consumer price index [CPI] or growth in average market incomes), since indexation during the period considered was rather ad hoc in the four countries.

The broader distributional effects of the crisis between years t and t − 1 (capturing together the effects of changes in policies, market incomes and employment status) are modelled by comparing the distribution of household disposable income in year t with that in year t − 1.

It is important to note that changes in employment incomes may on occasion be directly attributable to government policies, as in the case of changes in minimum wage legislation. However, we have not been able to disentangle these effects from the broader distributional impact of the crisis.

## Results

*Poverty*

We assess poverty effects using two different indicators. The first is the relative poverty rate, measured in terms of the proportion of the population with disposable income below 60 per cent of median. By construction, the relative poverty line goes up as median incomes improve, and down as median incomes fall. Needless to say, the significant fall in median incomes has been *the* defining characteristic of the Great Recession: in 2009–13 that estimated fall was massive in Greece (−36 per cent in real terms), but was also substantial in Portugal (−14 per cent), Spain (−11 per cent) and to a lesser extent Italy (−6 per cent).

To approximate the resulting sense of impoverishment, our second indicator fixes ('anchors') the poverty line at 60 per cent of the median of the 2009 income distribution, in real terms. By doing so, it reports the proportion of population who were unable to purchase in 2010–13 the goods and services that were just affordable to those with poverty line incomes in 2009.

The evolution of relative and anchored poverty rates in 2009–13 is shown in Figures 1 and 2 and, in greater detail, in Table 1.

Estimated relative poverty levels for the entire population moved up steadily in Greece, being 3.3 ppts higher in 2013 than in 2009. Relative poverty rates in the other three countries went up as well as down, the size of change being generally small. As might have been expected, changes in anchored poverty were more remarkable. In Greece, the proportion of population with incomes in 2013 below the 2009 poverty line (in real terms) was over 45 per cent, i.e. a dramatic increase by more than 25 ppts. The magnitude of change was smaller in Portugal (+6.3 ppts), Spain (+4.5 ppts) and Italy (+3.0 ppts).

Changes in sex- and age-specific relative poverty rates reveal interesting patterns. On the whole, they were less unfavourable for women than for men. In terms of age,

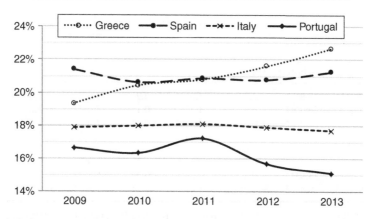

**Figure 1** Relative Poverty (2009–13)
*Source*: EUROMOD version G1.0.
*Note*: Proportion of population below the relative poverty threshold, set at 60 per cent of median equivalised disposable income.

the most remarkable finding is that relative poverty rates for the elderly (aged over 65) decreased very considerably in Greece, Spain and Portugal (by around five ppts or more), as well as in Italy (even though by less). On the other hand, relative poverty for young people (aged 18–29) went up in all four south European countries (especially in Greece and Spain). Poverty rates also went up for the 0–17 and the 30–64 age groups in Greece. This is because older people on low incomes, though not fully

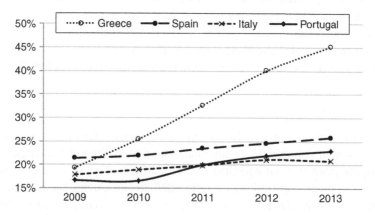

**Figure 2** Anchored Poverty (2009–13)
*Source*: EUROMOD version G1.0.
*Note*: Proportion of population below a fixed poverty threshold, set at 60 per cent of the 2009 median equivalised disposable income, adjusted for inflation. Adjustment based on the harmonised index of consumer prices (accessed on 19 December 2013); values for 2013 based on the European Commission Spring 2013 forecast (http://ec.europa.eu/economy_finance/eu/forecasts/2013_spring/statistical_en.pdf).

**Table 1** Changes in Relative and Anchored Poverty by Sex and Age (2013 vs. 2009)

| | Greece | | Spain | | Italy | | Portugal | |
|---|---|---|---|---|---|---|---|---|
| | Relative | Anchored | Relative | Anchored | Relative | Anchored | Relative | Anchored |
| All | 3.3*** | 25.8*** | − 0.2 | 4.5*** | − 0.2 | 3.0*** | − 1.5*** | 6.3*** |
| Men | 4.4*** | 26.5*** | 0.2 | 4.7*** | 0.1 | 3.0*** | − 1.2** | 6.1*** |
| Women | 2.3** | 25.2*** | − 0.5 | 4.3*** | − 0.4* | 3.0*** | − 1.9*** | 6.5*** |
| 0–17 | 3.2*** | 25.9*** | 0.6 | 5.6*** | − 0.2 | 3.5*** | − 1.2 | 7.2*** |
| 18–29 | 7.2*** | 32.4*** | 3.0*** | 8.9*** | 1.0* | 3.7*** | 1.0 | 6.8*** |
| 30–44 | 6.3*** | 25.9*** | 0.1 | 4.2*** | 0.2 | 2.9*** | − 0.7 | 5.9*** |
| 45–64 | 5.4*** | 25.9*** | 0.4 | 5.0*** | − 0.2 | 2.1*** | − 1.5** | 5.8*** |
| 65 + | − 6.3*** | 20.4*** | − 4.9*** | − 1.1*** | − 1.4*** | 3.5*** | − 5.1*** | 6.4*** |

*Source*: EUROMOD version G1.0, Distributive Analysis Stata Package (DASP) Version 2.3.
*Note*: Changes in relative and anchored poverty rates (2013 vs. 2009) in percentage points. Relative poverty rate defined as proportion of population below the relative poverty threshold, set at 60 per cent of median equivalised disposable income, using the OECD modified equivalence scale. Anchored poverty rate defined as proportion of population below a fixed poverty threshold, set at 60 per cent of the 2009 median equivalised disposable income, adjusted for inflation.
    Estimated changes marked as statistically significant at 90 per cent (*), 95 per cent (**) or 99 per cent confidence level (***). Information on the sample design of EU-SILC 2010 derived following Goedemé (2010).

protected, suffered lower income losses (e.g. cuts in pensions) than other groups (e.g. the unemployed). Note, however, that funding cuts and other changes in health care (not considered here) may have raised the costs of services and others barriers to access for those depending on them, among whom the elderly feature prominently.

The age groups experiencing the greatest increases in anchored poverty were the young (aged 18–29) in Greece, Spain and (by a smaller margin) Italy, and children (aged 0–17) in Portugal. Nevertheless, the elderly also suffered considerable increases in anchored poverty, except in Spain, where the relevant rate actually fell.

*Inequality*

We use two inequality indicators to determine whether the Great Recession has made the distribution of incomes more unequal. The first is the Gini coefficient, taking values ranging from 0 (total equality) to 1 (total inequality). The second inequality indicator is the income quintile share ratio S80/S20 (measuring the income share of the richest 20 per cent relative to that of the poorest 20 per cent). Note that the former is more sensitive to changes in the middle of the distribution, whereas the latter is more sensitive to changes at the two ends of the distribution.

As seen in Table 2, in 2009–13 the value of the Gini index increased very steeply in Greece (from 0.321 to 0.364, i.e. by 13 per cent). Elsewhere changes were not as large. Gini also went up a bit in Spain (in 2013), declined steadily in Portugal (in 2009–13) and hardly moved in Italy. In all three countries, differences, whether annual or cumulative, were rather small. The pattern was remarkably similar with respect to the

**Table 2** Inequality Indices (2009–13)

| | Greece | | Spain | | Italy | | Portugal | |
|---|---|---|---|---|---|---|---|---|
| | Gini | S80/S20 | Gini | S80/S20 | Gini | S80/S20 | Gini | S80/S20 |
| 2009 | 0.321 | 5.27 | 0.314 | 5.79 | 0.308 | 5.07 | 0.322 | 4.95 |
| 2010 | 0.328 | 5.57 | 0.314 | 5.75 | 0.312 | 5.25 | 0.320 | 4.90 |
| 2011 | 0.336 | 5.97 | 0.316 | 5.83 | 0.313 | 5.27 | 0.318 | 4.96 |
| 2012 | 0.354 | 7.02 | 0.314 | 5.80 | 0.313 | 5.25 | 0.311 | 4.70 |
| 2013 | 0.364 | 7.77 | 0.318 | 5.94 | 0.311 | 5.20 | 0.310 | 4.75 |

*Source*: EUROMOD version G1.0.

S80/S20 index. The income quintile share ratio went up very considerably in Greece (from 5.3 to 7.8, i.e. by 47 per cent). Changes in other countries were limited.

*Income Changes by Decile: Re-ranking Effects*

Over time, a considerable amount of re-ranking takes place, as a result of which the composition of income deciles changes. In Greece an estimated 65 per cent of the population moved income decile between 2009 and 2013; in Portugal and Spain that proportion was around 35 per cent, whereas in Italy only 18 per cent of the population were found in a different decile in 2013 relative to 2009.

In terms of composition, in 2013 relative to 2009, the poorest 20 per cent of the Greek population contained more unemployed workers (29 per cent vs. ten per cent), fewer elderly people (ten per cent vs. 18 per cent), and more city dwellers (40 per cent vs. 35 per cent). The bottom quintile also numbered more unemployed workers in Portugal (19 per cent vs. 13 per cent) and in Spain (16 per cent vs. eight per cent), and to a lesser extent in Italy (eight per cent vs. five per cent). Other changes were marginal.

The effects of re-ranking in real disposable household income are shown in Figure 3. These can be seen clearly taking the example of Greece, the country where income losses have been most dramatic. When deciles are fixed in 2009 (i.e. not allowing for re-ranking), we find that by 2013 those in the poorest ten per cent of the population in 2009 had lost a smaller-than-average proportion of their income (34 per cent vs. 36 per cent in real terms). On the other hand, if deciles are recalculated each year (i.e. allowing for re-ranking), we find that the income of those in the poorest ten per cent of the population in 2013 had fallen by as much as 69 per cent relative to the income of their counterparts in 2009 (i.e. those who occupied the lowest income decile in that year).

As seen in Figure 3, a similar pattern prevailed in Spain and Italy. In both countries, those in the bottom decile in 2009 had by 2013 lost a smaller proportion of their income than had those in the top decile in 2009. Nevertheless, allowing for re-ranking, the poorest ten per cent of the population in 2013 found themselves much poorer than the poorest ten per cent in 2009. True, the richest ten per cent of the population in these countries were also less rich in 2013 than the richest ten per cent were in 2009.

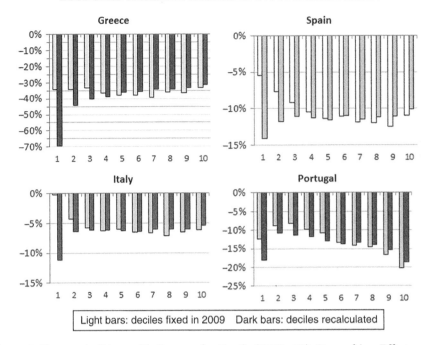

**Figure 3** Changes in Disposable Income by Decile (2009–13): Re-ranking Effects
*Source*: EUROMOD version G1.0.
*Note*: Household disposable income is equivalised according to the OECD modified equivalence scale and measured in real terms (i.e. adjusted for inflation). The charts are drawn to different scales, but the interval between gridlines is the same on each chart.

However, the decline of the poorest decile was greater than it was for the richest decile. The pattern was slightly different in Portugal, where income changes allowing for re-ranking were similar for the top and bottom deciles. Even there, the relative gain was greater when deciles were fixed in 2009 than when they were recalculated each year.

*Disentangling the First-Order Effects of Austerity Policies*

Have adverse distributional changes taken place *because* of the austerity policies introduced by governments? Or, as sometimes is argued, *in spite* of these policies? In other words, have fiscal consolidation packages been designed to minimise the impact of the recession on the weakest groups in society? Again, the political importance of this question is obvious. Can it be answered?

As a matter of fact, it can – provided we keep in mind that, as discussed previously, we only estimate *first-order* effects. In Figures 4 and 5 we attempt to estimate the yearly changes in anchored poverty and inequality caused by policies alone vs. overall effects (i.e. that also include the effects of changes in individuals' labour market status and market incomes). Crucially, we warn against interpreting the difference between these

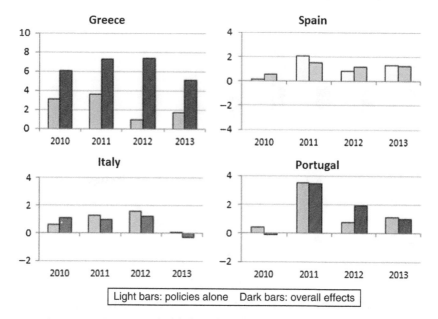

**Figure 4** Changes in Anchored Poverty Rates: First-order Effect of Policies vs. Overall Effect of the Crisis

*Source*: EUROMOD version G1.0, DASP Version 2.3.

*Note*: Changes in anchored poverty rates in percentage points. Anchored poverty rate defined as proportion of population below a fixed poverty threshold, set at 60 per cent of the 2009 median equivalised disposable income, adjusted for inflation. Estimated changes in poverty due to policies alone are statistically significant for all years in Greece and Portugal, in 2011–13 in Spain and in 2010–12 in Italy. Estimated changes in poverty due to the overall effect of the crisis are statistically significant for all years in Greece, Spain and Italy and in 2011–13 in Portugal (a = 0.05).

two estimates as equal to the (unobservable) broader economic developments over and above the effect of government policies (i.e. that would have occurred in the absence of changes in government policies). A detailed description of policy changes can be found in the Appendix (Tables A1–A4).

As seen in Figure 4, results varied significantly between countries. Our estimates suggest that in Greece about half of the total increase in anchored poverty in 2010 and 2011 can be attributed to the first-order effect of austerity policies; in 2012 and 2013 austerity policies explain a much smaller proportion of the total poverty increase (13 per cent and 33 per cent, respectively).

In Spain, austerity policies alone had a very limited effect on poverty in 2010. In contrast, in 2012 they explained more than 70 per cent of the total increase in anchored poverty. In 2010 and 2012 they raised anchored poverty more than the combination of policies with changes in the wider economy did.

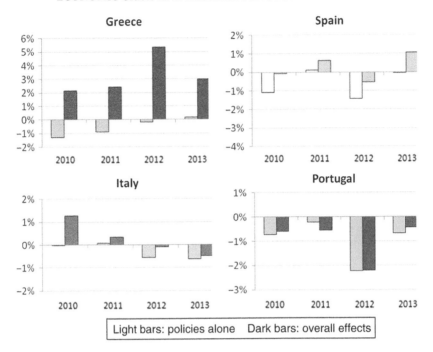

**Figure 5** Changes in the Gini Index: First-order Effect of Policies vs. Overall Effect of the Crisis
*Source*: EUROMOD version G1.0, DASP Version 2.3.
*Note*: Percentage year-on-year changes in the Gini index. Estimated changes in inequality due to policies alone are statistically significant for all years in Spain, in 2010–12 in Greece, in 2011–13 in Italy and in 2010 and 2012–13 in Portugal. Estimated changes in inequality due to the overall effect of the crisis are statistically significant for all years in Greece and Portugal, in 2011–13 in Spain and in 2010–11 and 2013 in Italy (a $=$ 0.05).

The latter was also the case in Italy (all years except 2010) and Portugal (all years except 2012). In these countries the combined effect of policies with broader economic developments was often negative (i.e. poverty-reducing).

Inequality effects, presented in Figure 5, were subtly different. In Greece and Spain the first-order effects of the policies pursued seem to have mostly compressed the income distribution, while the combined effect of policies with broader economic developments appears to have made it consistently more unequal, that pattern being stronger in Greece than in Spain. The picture was similar in Italy and Portugal, where changes in inequality were generally not as great, with the inequality-reducing (first-order) effect of policies being occasionally rather strong (as in Portugal in 2012).

*Identifying the Effect of Individual Policies on Inequality*

That some austerity policies *per se* may have actually reduced inequality seems at odds with established views about what is going on in the countries most affected by the crisis. In fact, our finding seems to be the combined effect of two opposing tendencies: some policies distributed the burden of austerity fairly and/or affected groups located towards the top of the income distribution, while other policies cut incomes across the board and/or affected low-income households more.

Tax–benefit policies are grouped under four headings: public sector pay; taxes and social insurance contributions (SICs); pensions and related policies; and other social benefits. Note that, although this grouping was necessary in order to render the analysis manageable, bundling some policies under the same heading will inevitably offset some of them against each other, obfuscating policy options and their distributional effects.

We then formally assess the first-order impact of each policy bundle on inequality by calculating the percentage change between the value of the Gini index if the policy bundle in question had remained as in year t − 1 relative to its actual value after the implementation of the policy in year t. Positive (negative) values indicate that *ceteris paribus* the policy in question rendered the income distribution less (more) equal. We use the term 'progressive' (or 'regressive') interchangeably with 'inequality-reducing' (or, respectively, 'inequality-enhancing'). The results are shown in Table 3.

It can be seen clearly that the impact of many policy changes, though no doubt significant for the groups affected, was actually quite negligible in terms of the distribution of incomes as a whole. The partial exceptions were as follows.

**Table 3** Inequality Effects of Policy Changes

| | Change in the Gini index (%) | | | |
|---|---|---|---|---|
| | 2010 | 2011 | 2012 | 2013 |
| Greece | | | | |
| public sector pay | − 0.57 | − 0.10 | − 0.31 | − 0.52 |
| taxes / SIC | − 0.84 | − 0.13 | 0.07 | 0.98 |
| pensions and related policies | − 0.30 | − 0.06 | − 0.41 | 0.90 |
| other social benefits | 0.35 | -0.16 | 0.25 | − 1.47 |
| Spain | | | | |
| public sector pay | − 0.12 | − 0.12 | − 0.23 | n.a. |
| taxes / SICs | − 0.47 | 0.04 | − 1.11 | − 0.02 |
| pensions and related policies | − 0.06 | − 0.04 | − 0.04 | − 0.02 |
| other social benefits | − 0.30 | − 0.01 | − 0.23 | 0.07 |
| Italy | | | | |
| public sector pay | 0.06 | 0.00 | 0.02 | 0.01 |
| taxes / SICs | 0.01 | − 0.52 | − 0.42 | 0.00 |
| pensions and related policies | 0.00 | 0.00 | − 0.01 | 0.00 |
| other social benefits | − 0.04 | − 0.06 | − 0.06 | − 0.20 |
| Portugal | | | | |
| public sector pay | n.a. | − 0.53 | − 1.04 | 0.96 |
| taxes / SICs | − 0.39 | − 1.93 | − 0.60 | − 3.67 |
| pensions and related policies | − 0.16 | − 0.01 | − 1.15 | 0.69 |
| other social benefits | − 0.18 | 1.97 | − 0.13 | 1.15 |

*Source*: EUROMOD version G1.0.
*Note*: Percentage changes in the Gini index. 'n.a.' indicates no policy changes between the two years.

Cuts in public sector pay seem to have been progressive, especially in Greece (in particular in 2010 and 2013). This was also the case in Portugal (in 2011–12), where the reversal of pay cuts in 2013 seems to have had a regressive effect. This effect mostly stems from the fact that, as a combination of steady employment and assortative mating, civil servants tend to be located at the upper end of the income distribution.

The first-order effect of changes in direct taxes and SICs seemed mostly to have rendered the income distribution less unequal (*ceteris paribus*). This was especially so in Portugal in 2011, but also in Greece (2010), Spain (2010 and 2012) and Italy (2011). In contrast, the 2013 tax and SIC changes in Greece appeared to have the opposite effect.

Pension cuts and related policies (such as the special levies) appear to have had a more mixed distributional impact. Some of these changes were progressive, as in Portugal (in 2012) and to a lesser extent in Greece (in 2010 and 2012). This effect mostly resulted from the design of these measures, which partly or fully protected those on low incomes. On the other hand, the across-the-board pension cuts in Greece, and the restoration of the 13th and 14th pension payments in Portugal, both in 2013, appear to have had significantly regressive effects.

Examples of changes in social benefits having a progressive distributional effect were few and far between. We may mention here the (late) introduction of a means-tested child benefit scheme in Greece (in 2013). By contrast, reductions in the generosity of minimum income in Portugal (in 2011 and 2013) obviously had a regressive impact.

## Conclusions

We set out to estimate the distributional impact of the Great Recession in four southern European countries. Our results can be summarised as follows.

To start with, Greece clearly stands out from the other three countries considered here. As a result of the current crisis, poverty and inequality there have risen to alarming levels. In some of the other countries, for instance in Portugal and Spain, where median incomes declined considerably, anchored poverty (by reference to a poverty line fixed to its 2009 level in real terms) also went up, though by much less than in Greece. Our findings with respect to relative poverty and inequality were less straightforward, improvements alternating with deteriorations and little overall change (again, except in Greece).

On the whole, the Great Recession seems to have changed the composition of the population in poverty. Those at the bottom of the income distribution are younger than before the crisis, and more likely to be unemployed (or on low pay) than pensioners. As a result of that, income changes are less pronounced when deciles are fixed as in the base year (in this case, 2009) than when they are recalculated each year. Indeed, allowing for re-ranking makes it more evident that those at the bottom of the income distribution today are considerably poorer than those occupying the same position before the outbreak of the current crisis.

We have also attempted to clarify the various interactions between government policies, growth and income distribution. Specifically, tax–benefit policies act both directly (through their effect on the distribution of incomes) and indirectly (through their effects on aggregate demand, and hence on firms and workers, i.e. on jobs and wages). As a result of these interactions, the full effects of tax–benefit policies cannot be reduced to the first-order effects estimated here.

Having said that, isolating the effects on poverty and inequality of tax–benefit policies *per se* from the overall impact of the crisis is of some interest, as it may help identify policies that minimise adverse distributional effects while reducing budget deficits. In fact, some of the policies considered here seem to have had a more progressive first-order effect than others. This may be because special care was taken to make a particular policy 'fair' by design. Alternatively, it may stem from the fact that those adversely affected tended to be located towards the top of the income distribution.

While the impact of policies on inequality can be described as moderate (or even equality-reducing), this is far from saying that fiscal adjustment programmes have been a success in overall distributional terms. Our estimates suggest that in most of the countries examined here poverty increased, and the policies implemented accounted for a major part of that increase. In some cases policies alone raised anchored poverty more than the combined effect of policies and changes in the wider economy did.

A certain amount of caution is called for in interpreting our results. The main issues, to do either with our approach or with our assumptions, are briefly discussed below.

Accounting for tax evasion and non-take-up of social benefits is limited to some of the countries considered here. Clearly, a more uniform treatment of these would enhance the comparability and credibility of our findings. The same holds for the treatment of indirect taxation, ignored here. Given the relative weight of indirect taxes in many tax systems, estimating their distributional impact would greatly enhance the accuracy of our results.

On another note, while austerity policies may adversely affect what was once called the 'social wage', benefits in kind are ignored here. This issue has been addressed in the context of EUROMOD (Paulus, Sutherland & Tsakloglou 2010; Verbist & Matsaganis 2014). However, we still know too little about the actual effect of funding cuts on the quality and quantity of social services. Collecting the relevant information, and relating inputs to outputs, would require a substantial amount of further research – but the gains from that could be substantial.

Although significant progress has been made towards accounting for macro-economic aspects of the crisis, much remains to do to capture the impact of the recession more fully. Examples include modelling wage dynamics across sectors and occupations, capturing additional labour market transitions (such as from full-time to part-time employment) and adjusting for demographic changes, especially in countries where the crisis has led to significant migration flows.

While we are fully aware that these weaknesses affect the accuracy of our results, we are confident that our research offers a good approximation of the first-order distributional impact of austerity policies and the wider impact of the crisis in the four countries considered here. Given the topicality of the questions addressed, and the public interest in the answers, we believe that work based on microsimulation is a good alternative to waiting until future waves of official statistics are released. Furthermore, if the research question involves identifying the effect of different changes taking place at the same time, distinguishing between progressive and regressive items within the same policy package (as is the case here), there is no alternative to microsimulation.

In our paper we have attempted to link the literature on the effects of fiscal consolidation on growth, including the analysis of fiscal multipliers, with that on its effects on inequality and poverty. We have noted that the static effects of fiscal consolidation policies may be at odds with their dynamic effects. Clearly, however, we still know too little to quantify the size and direction of the dynamic (second-order) effects of austerity on inequality via growth. More research into that interaction would enable us to identify policies that promote both growth and equality, even while the room for fiscal policy remains limited.

## Acknowledgements

We would like to thank Andrea Brandolini, Francesco Figari, Tim Goedemé, Isabelle Maquet, Alari Paulus and Holly Sutherland for insightful discussions of earlier versions of the paper. We are also grateful for valuable comments to Bea Cantillon, Ana Guillén, Rodolfo Gutiérrez, John Hills, Gilles Mourre, Maria Petmesidou, Karel Van den Bosch and other participants at conferences in Amsterdam (June 2013), Brussels (November 2013), Washington (March 2014) and Antwerp (April 2014), where previous versions were presented. Our research is financially supported by the European Union Seventh Framework Programme (FP7/2012–2016) under grant agreement n° 290613 (ImPRovE project). The views expressed in this paper are those of the authors. The usual disclaimer applies.

## References

Agnello, L. & Sousa, R. M. (2012) 'Fiscal adjustments and income inequality: a first assessment', *Applied Economics Letters*, vol. 19, no. 16, pp. 1627–1632.

Ahren, R., Arnold, J. & Moeser, C. (2011) 'The sharing of macroeconomic risk: who loses (and gains) from macroeconomic shocks?' OECD Economics Department Working Paper No. 877, OECD Publishing.

Alcidi, C. & Gros, D. (2012) 'Why is the Greek economy collapsing? A simple tale of high multipliers and low exports', CEPS Commentary, Centre for European Policy Studies, Brussels.

Alesina, A. & Ardagna, S. (2012) 'The design of fiscal adjustments', NBER Working Paper 18423.

Alesina, A., Favero, C. & Giavazzi, F. (2012) 'The output effects of fiscal consolidations', NBER Working Paper 18336.

Auerbach, A. J. & Gorodnichenko, Y. (2012) 'Measuring the output responses to fiscal policy', *American Economic Journal: Economic Policy*, vol. 4, no. 2, pp. 1–27.

Avram, S., Figari, F., Leventi, C., Levy, H., Navicke, E., Matsaganis, M., Militaru, E., Paulus, A., Rastringina, O. & Sutherland, H. (2013) 'The distributional effects of austerity measures: a comparison of nine EU countries', EUROMOD Working Paper EM2/13, ISER, University of Essex.

Ball, L., Furceri, D., Leigh, D. & Loungani, P. (2013) 'The distributional effects of fiscal austerity', IMF Working Paper 13/151.

Ball, L., Leigh, D. & Loungani, P. (2011) 'Painful medicine', *Finance and Development*, vol. 48, no. 3, pp. 20–23.

Bargain, O. & Callan, T. (2010) 'Analysing the effects of tax–benefit reforms on income distribution: a decomposition approach', *The Journal of Economic Inequality*, vol. 8, no. 1, pp. 1–21.

Bargain, O., Callan, T., Doorley, K. & Keane, C. (2013) 'Changes in income distributions and the role of tax–benefit policy during the great recession: An international perspective', IZA Discussion Paper 7737.

Barro, R. J. (1990) 'Government spending in a simple model of endogeneous growth', *Journal of Political Economy*, vol. 98, no. 5, pp. S103–S126.

Bontout, O. & Lokajickova, T. (2013) 'Social protection budgets in the crisis in the EU', European Commission DG EMPL Working Paper 1/2013, Publications Office of the European Union, Luxembourg.

Bourguignon, F., Bussolo, M. & Da Silva, L. P. (2008) 'The impact of macro-economic policies on poverty and income distribution Macro-Micro Evaluation Techniques and Tools', The World Bank and Palgrave-Macmillan, New York.

Brandolini, A., D'Amuri, F. & Faiella, I. (2013) 'Country case study – Italy', in *The Great Recession and the Distribution of Household Income*, eds S. P. Jenkins, A. Brandolini, J. Micklewright & B. Nolan, Oxford University Press, Oxford.

Brewer, M., Browne, J. & Joyce, R. (2011) 'Child and working-age poverty from 2010 to 2020', IFS Commentary C121, Institute for Fiscal Studies, London.

Browne, J. & Levell, P. (2010) 'The distributional effect of tax and benefit reforms to be introduced between June 2010 and April 2014: a revised assessment', IFS Briefing Note 108, Institute for Fiscal Studies, London.

Callan, T., Nolan, B. & Walsh, J. (2011) 'The economic crisis, public sector pay, and the income distribution', in *Who Loses in the Downturn? Economic Crisis, Employment and Income Distribution*, eds H. Immervoll, A. Peichl & K. Tatsiramos, vol. 32, Research in Labour Economics, Emerald Group Publishing Limited, Bingley, pp. 207–225.

Corsetti, G. J., Meier, A. & Müller, G. (2012) 'What determines government spending multipliers?', *Economic Policy*, vol. 27, no. 72, pp. 521–565.

Dolls, M., Fuest, C. & Peichl, A. (2012) 'Automatic stabilizers and economic crisis: US vs. Europe', *Journal of Public Economics*, vol. 96, no. 3–4, pp. 279–294.

EC. (2012) 'European Economic Forecast Autumn 2012', European Economy 8/2012, European Commission, Publications Office of the European Union, Luxembourg.

ECB. (2012) 'Monthly Bulletin December 2012', European Central Bank, Frankfurt am Main.

EUROMOD. (2014) 'Country Reports', available online at: https://www.iser.essex.ac.uk/euromod/resources-for-euromod-users/country-reports

Eurostat. Online statistics database (last accessed: March 2014), Eurostat, Luxemburg (2014).

Eyraud, L. & Weber, A. (2013) 'The challenge of debt reduction during fiscal consolidation', IMF Working Paper 13/67.

Goedemé, T. (2010) 'The standard error of estimates based on EU-SILC. An exploration through the Europe 2020 poverty indicators', Working Paper 10/09, Herman Deleeck Centre for Social Policy, University of Antwerp.

Goujard, A. (2013) 'Cross-country spillovers from fiscal consolidation', OECD Economics Department Working Paper No. 1099, OECD Publishing.

IMF. (2012) 'World Economic Outlook: coping with high debt and sluggish growth', Washington.

Jenkins, S. P., Brandolini, A., Micklewright, J. & Nolan, B. (2013) *The Great Recession and the Distribution of Household Income*, Oxford University Press, Oxford.

Jordà, Ò. & Taylor, A. M. (2013) 'The time for austerity: estimating the average treatment effect of fiscal policy', Paper presented at the NBER Summer Institute.

Joyce, R. & Sibieta, L. (2013) 'Country case study – UK', in *The Great Recession and the Distribution of Household Income*, eds S. P. Jenkins, A. Brandolini, J. Micklewright & B. Nolan, Oxford University Press, Oxford.

Koutsampelas, C. & Policarpou, A. (2013) 'Austerity and the income distribution: the case of Cyprus', EUROMOD Working Paper EM4/13, ISER, University of Essex.

Leventi, C. & Matsaganis, M. (2013) 'Distributional implications of the crisis in Greece in 2009-2012', EUROMOD Working Paper EM14/13, ISER, University of Essex.

Leventi, C., Navicke, J., Rastrigina, O., Sutherland, H., Ozdemir, E. & Ward, T. (2013) 'Nowcasting: estimating developments in the risk of poverty and income distribution in 2012 and 2013', Research Note 1/2013, Social Situation Monitor, European Commission.

Nolan, B., Callan, T. & Maître, B. (2013) 'Country case study – Ireland', in *The Great Recession and the Distribution of Household Income*, eds S. P. Jenkins, A. Jenkins, J. Micklewright & B. Nolan, Oxford University Press, Oxford.

OECD. (2013) 'How much scope for growth and equity-friendly fiscal consolidation?', OECD Economics Department Policy Notes No. 20, July 2013.

OECD. (2014) 'OECD forecasts during and after the financial crisis: a post mortem', OECD Economics Department Policy Notes No. 23, February 2014.

Paulus, A., Sutherland, H. & Tsakloglou, P. (2010) 'The distributional impact of in-kind public benefits in European countries', *Journal of Policy Analysis and Management*, vol. 29, no. 2, pp. 243–266.

Romer, C. D. & Romer, D. H. (2010) 'The macroeconomic effects of tax changes: estimates based on a new measure of fiscal shocks', *American Economic Review*, vol. 100, no. 3, pp. 763–801.

Salgado, M. F., Figari, F., Sutherland, H. & Tumino, A. (2014) 'Welfare compensation for unemployment in the Great Recession', *Review of Income and Wealth*, vol. 60, no. S1, pp. S177–S204.

Sutherland, H. & Figari, F. (2013) 'EUROMOD: the European Union tax–benefit microsimulation model', *International Journal of Microsimulation*, vol. 6, no. 1, pp. 4–26.

Verbist, G. & Matsaganis, M. (2014) 'The redistributive capacity of services in the EU', in *Reconciling Work and Poverty Reduction: How Successful are European Welfare States?* eds B. Cantillon & F. Vandenbroucke, Oxford University Press, Oxford.

Woo, J., Bova, E., Kinda, T. & Zhang, Y. S. (2013) 'Distributional consequences of fiscal consolidation and the role of fiscal policy: what do the data say?' IMF Working Paper 13/195, Washington.

## Appendix

An Online Appendix is available for this article which can be accessed via the online version of this journal available at: http://dx.doi.org/ 10.1080/13608746.2014.947700

# Index

Note: Page numbers in **bold** type refer to figures
Page numbers in *italic* type refer to tables
Page numbers followed by 'n' refer to notes

For Product Safety Concerns and Information please contact our EU
representative GPSR@taylorandfrancis.com Taylor & Francis Verlag GmbH,
Kaufingerstraße 24, 80331 München, Germany


Printed and bound by CPI Group (UK) Ltd, Croydon, CR0 4YY
08/05/2025
01864325-0005